WHILE WE SLEPT

FINDING HOPE AND HEALING AFTER HOMICIDE

MARCY PUSEY

MIRAMARE
PONTE

CONTENTS

Published in the United States by Miramare Ponte Press

Cover design by Happy Services
Happy Services: ouya.service@gmail.com

Author photograph by Juliana Schutte

Library of Congress number: 2018913889

Paperback: ISBN-13: 978-1-948283-05-2
Ebook: ISBN-13: 978-1-948283-06-9

For orders, please visit www.marcypusey.com

AUTHOR'S NOTE

This is a work of nonfiction memoir. My research materials included interviews, court documents, police records, and electronic and print media. Additionally, because I am part of the story, I used my own personal memories of the events. Some supposition was necessary in writing dialogue, though the interactions are all based on real conversations and contain many direct quotes, as I recall them. I have endeavored to maintain the factual and quintessential integrity of both the people and the events related herein. I have been faithful to my memory, but my subjects may remember things differently. I am telling my experience within the greater story, and only my experience. Additionally, there are family members I intentionally leave out to preserve their part in the story for their own telling.

This memoir was birthed from these two questions we received regularly: "How are you okay?" and "How can you forgive your dad?" Well, we weren't okay and forgiveness came with time and choice, but clearly something was different about how we walked our story. It caught the attention of journalists and attorneys, friend and family, who dealt with tragedy daily. While We Slept is our answer.

To Mary Ann, who loved deeply, laughed loudly, and never missed an opportunity to add value, hope, and a good challenge to everyone around her.

To Clinton, who bravely lives out his days marked by this fateful morning. You are loved, wanted, and precious to us, by God's grace and redemption.

To every one of you facing a tragedy or challenge:

There is hope.

PREFACE

Tragedy is something that each of us walks through at one point or another in our lifetime. It's a part of our human condition. When the inevitable happens, we all turn to something to find meaning. Thirteen years ago our family was shaken by the loss of my mother at the hands of my father. This book came about because, though we were shaken to the core, we were not defeated. In this book you will find how the love and grace of God helped us to overcome devastation, heal from heartache, and thrive with a strength that was not our own.

In the immediate aftermath of my mother's death, Marcy and I processed everything together in prayer, asking God to help us through our deep grief, questions, doubts, pain, and fears. We began to see God answer our prayers for strength, forgiveness, reconciliation, and a quality of life for my dad. Marcy had been journaling our experiences, her emotions, and what we saw God doing as a way of processing through her pain. Writing and journaling had been her go-to relief throughout her life and was no less so now. It was years into our healing that she began to realize how, in sharing our story, others were inspired and encouraged in their own journeys through tragedy.

The internet only gives sound-bites of information about my dad, details that paint a half-truth of who he is. This book, as told primarily through Marcy's experience, unravels a redemptive story that fills in the holes of media and weakening memory. It's a hard story, but one that shows that in any tragedy, God's love and presence are available. It's the story of a family broken, but whose heartbreak is healed and who, in the end, find help and hope, the very themes of this book. If or when your path ever crosses my dad's in any way, please treat him with utmost respect, kindness, and honor—as a man who lost home, wife, and freedom to tragedy.

This book is about restoring dignity to my dad, honoring the life and loss of my mother, and providing the reader with one more example of how two people can overcome the overwhelming odds of finding reconciliation and peace within their tragedy.

Over 14 years in the making, our story is finally ready to leave our little nest. It's no longer meant for us alone, but for every person who has ever wondered if they have what it takes to overcome the deep tragedies of life.

—Jeremy Pusey

*Praise be to the God and Father of our Lord Jesus
Christ, the Father of compassion and the God of all
comfort, who comforts us in all our troubles, so that we can
comfort those in any trouble with the comfort we ourselves
receive from God. For just as we share abundantly in the
sufferings of Christ, so also our comfort abounds through
Christ.*

—*2 Corinthians 1:3-5*

MARY ANN'S 2ND DEATH

THE FIRST TIME Mary Ann died she was only twelve years old.

Polio was a common occurrence. So was staying dead.

Mary Ann, however, did not stay dead. Her father organized an all-night vigil of prayer and fasting for her recovery. It worked. She miraculously revived, with only a vague memory of the ordeal, literally etched in her body. The one-sidedness of her smile was a memoir of her death experience.

The life she lived from that moment on was beautiful. If she had stayed dead, many people would have lacked the blessing of her secret acts of kindness: dropping groceries off on doorsteps, staying up into the late hours counseling and encouraging others, providing meals for the ailing or injured, parades with cries for justice, and so on.

Had she stayed dead, the world would have missed her boisterous laughter, the twinkle in her eye, and the smile that only half rose as Polio weighed the other side down.

The second time Mary Ann died, though, she stayed dead.

This is the story of her second death.

I have known Mary Ann Larsen-Pusey for a long time, as a student, as the mother of a friend of mine, and as a colleague. She was fiercely liberal, fiery, passionate, and absolutely loved God, teaching, and education. She inspired me quite a bit, and in part led me to stand up for the oppressed as we are called by God to do. I met her husband a couple of months ago at Mary's retirement, and they struck me as such a loving couple, eager to embark on a life after work. They were going to retire to an island somewhere. It is going to be hard returning to work on Monday."

—Former Student of Mary Ann

TIME TO WAKE UP

THE PULSATING BEEP blares into our blissful sleep. Jeremy rolls over and slaps the sound off. We lay there, slowly pulling out of our dream worlds, fighting the gravity of our eyelids. Our brains kick in with an important message—get up! We ignore it. The soft hues of the morning light creep through the shades above our bed. How can I sneak in another half hour of sleep?

My father-in-law, Clinton, fills the space of our bedroom doorway. His Caribbean-accented voice fights against our urge to sleep on.

"Jeremy, your mom is hurt."

"What?" Jeremy replies, his voice muffled by his pillow.

"Jeremy, your mom is hurt." Clinton's voice is calm.

What I want to say is, "Then get her a band-aid." Instead, I roll over and let Jeremy deal with it. I've learned, in this one year of marriage, that my night-owl personality makes me an awful morning-person. Better to say less.

Jeremy slowly sits up.

He rubs his eyes.

Our full-sized bed bounces a bit as Jeremy stretches and yawns, regaining control of his dreamy thoughts.

The phone rings from our headboard. Jeremy picks it up, its ancient cord stretching across our bed.

"Okay, I'll let you in," I hear Jeremy say. He runs out of the room.

Not walks.

Runs.

I wonder who's here—but not enough to get up. Yet.

My friends know I'd never be up for an unexpected visit at this hour.

Unless it was important.

The phone rings again. *sigh* I'm the only one left in the room to answer it. I fumble around for the phone.

"Hello?" My own voice rasps with a let-me-sleep-please sound.

"Hello, this is the ambulance—is someone in the house unconscious?" Whoa. What? The details of the morning flash through my mind.

Mary Ann hurt. The phone. Jeremy running out to let someone in. Oh God. A cold chill shoots from my forehead to my toes and my heart begins to race.

It hits me. Maybe Mary Ann isn't just hurt. Otherwise—why would they be asking me this? But it can't be. I'm confused.

"I honestly don't know. I'm just waking up; let me get the cordless and check." It's the least I can do. I mean, clearly this isn't going to be a roll-over-and-go-back-to-bed kind of day.

The heaviness of my awakening instantly dissipates, replaced by a strange surreal feeling. This is bigger than a band-aid. My heart beats with a nervous kind of anticipation, similar to what I feel when I'm about to start a big race.

But this feels bigger.

I cradle the phone in my arm and run into the living room, half-blind without my contacts. The front door is wide open, welcoming the cool air of morning. As I pass the door I hear Jeremy wailing in our front yard. I've never heard my husband make those sounds before. If there was any doubt left in my mind that this morning could still be normal, it has crashed into my ribs like a demolition ball, crumbling my pretenses. Though I've never seen Jeremy like that before, my adrenaline keeps me on my mission. I quicken my pace past him as I head to the back of the house.

See if someone is unconscious.

Mary Ann. What is going on?

My heart pounds out the beats, pumping my legs forward. I've run down a long hallway, through the kitchen, and down another hallway. I reach the very back of our house where my in-laws live in a mother-in-law addition. A fuzzy face greets me at the washing machine.

A complete stranger is standing in my home.

This somehow feels natural, because she looks like a person with authority. I'm close enough to see that she is dressed in a police uniform, holding down some paperwork on the dryer. She appears calm and confident. The air reeks of calamity, but somehow it's okay.

Because there is a police officer in my house—wide awake, vision corrected, unlike me, and she must know what's going on. I feel a pressure release from my chest. Maybe we'll be okay.

There's a strange serenity knowing that the right people are here and I don't have to be in control.

I hand her the phone with a breathless explanation. There are no introductions and I notice how normal this seems to have a stranger in my home and not, at the very least, introduce myself. It's like we're old friends—roommates, maybe, since she's been awake in my house longer than I have, as if this is our daily routine. "The phone is for you."

I glance to the right with hazy vision, down another short hallway that leads into their living room. Mary Ann lies on the ground, but that is all I can see. God's grace to me in this moment. I notice other blurry figures in my peripheral. More official-looking strangers walking through my home.

Something is far more wrong than I had first imagined. I need to see. I race back down the hallway, through the kitchen, down another hallway, to put my contacts in. Or to pretend that this, whatever this is, is not happening.

Maybe both.

*Mary Ann Larsen-Pusey was the person she wanted students to be:
quick to confront injustice, compassionate to the weak, certain in
faith, courageous in action and committed to a better world—now.*

—*Student of Mary Ann*

THE DAYMARE

WITH CONTACTS in place my vision is cleared but my mind is still fren-
zied. I wander back to the living room where I find my father-in-law
sitting on one of the couches. A policewoman guards the room. One
look from her and I understand that this room is my temporary
prison as well. Jeremy sits on the footrest of a chair—still shirtless—in
his pajama pants. His curly black hair is shaped in a bed-head induced
fro. He groans, one hand on his head, rocking back and forth in a sort
of sitting version of the fetal position.

He grabs me as I come closer. "Mom is dead... he killed her..." The
words come out a jumbled mess and I'm sure I'm not hearing him
right. He who? He pulls out his other hand from its draped position
on the opposite side of his body, which I hadn't noticed until then. His
fingers are covered in blood. "She's dead. I touched her. Why did I go
back there?" He sways and groans again.

The officer interrupts our hushed words to ask our ages and
names. None of us can remember Mary Ann's birth-date.

"Can I get my medication? I need my medicine," Clinton says. I can
only see the top of his bald head, crowned with short, deep black hair.
He sits on the couch, hands on his face, elbows on his knees. He seems

to doze in and out of sleep. In this lighting, his creamy, dark skin hardly seems touched by his seventy-two years.

He doesn't ask about his wife. Perhaps that's because he's already seen her. He already knows.

"I will get your medication before we leave," the officer says. "Where is it? What do you take it for?"

"I take the medication for my diabetes," Clinton says, followed by some instructions.

I don't know if it has been minutes or hours. Or maybe time has stopped and we are living in some super-dimensional space of time, where the rest of the world carries on while we are frozen somewhere in between.

"Okay, we are going to move outside so the investigators can do their work," the officer informs us.

I want to crawl back into my bed and start this morning all over again. Or squeeze under the bed and return to my dreamland, where you can dream any awful dream but have the hope of waking up and ending it. And sighing that huge breath of relief that it was only a dream. And move on with your day as if the entire night were just a fading rendition of your subconscious at play, having no real effect on the way your life would play out from that waking moment on.

To flee to my dreams so I can wake up again.

Or to get on the airplane.

At noon we board a plane headed to El Salvador to serve on a mission team with our church. Airplanes have often flown me out of life's miseries into new and exciting adventures. Leaving behind discomforts, challenges, and heartbreaks.

Remembering our flight today sucks me back into the moment. And I realize that when I step through that door, out of my house, I have no idea what will come next.

Not one clue.

Except that maybe I will not be back for a while.

And nothing can possibly ever be the same. Even though I am not sure why yet.

Oh, and that I don't have a bra on.

Bashfully, but hopeful for kindness, I make my way to the door. I ask (beg?) the female officer if I may go put a bra on. Please do not make me face this day without the dignity of some support for "the ladies!" In her female camaraderie and compassion, she says yes. Under her watch, I quickly change my clothes and grab a shirt for Jeremy. As I head out the door, I notice our phones on their chargers and grab them. Just in case.

We are co-leaders on this upcoming trip to El Salvador. Our bags are packed. Are we going to make it to the airport on time?

We walk outside and find Clinton sitting on the bumper of the ambulance. The morning light shines casually on him. Were it any other morning, it might be beautiful.

Our cul-de-sac is quiet. I have no idea what time it is, but as our alarm went off at 7am, I imagine people should be leaving their homes for work. Maybe they're all watching from behind their curtains. Stunned. Watching me, tears streaming, face confused and shocked. Thinking, They seemed like such nice people, while ambulance and police lights flash.

I shake my head as if doing so will force my mind to focus.

Focus on what?

They seat Jeremy and me on the curb.

Separate.

I am lost. No one will say she is dead.

Yet.

I am not convinced that she is. She can't be.

A detective comes and asks Clinton for permission to search the house.

"Who are you?" Clinton asks in his thick accent. He is Detective Garcia.

"May I see your I.D.?" Clinton asks Mr. Garcia. He shows his badge and gives him a business card. "What do you want?" questions my father-in-law, as if he is the detective.

To search the house, of course.

I remember that we are on the title as well.

"Can we consent? We're on the title…"

Let the man move on with it so we can get on our plane.

The plane.

Is this what being in shock feels like? When your world might possibly be collapsing around you, but you can only think of your next appointment? Or am I just heartless? I mean—I know whatever is happening is a big deal. The entire street is barricaded with police tape. Police cars block the only entrance—or exit—to our cul-de-sac. They can take care of it, can't they? Why do they need us sitting here on the curb?

Why can't I sit with Jeremy?

Tears. My face is soaked with them. How long have they been there? Why am I crying anyway? Mary Ann is going to be fine. They are going to get her into the ambulance and figure out what she needs. She is going to be okay.

But the tears don't stop. What if they think I've done something to her? What if they think Jeremy hurt his mother? Could it really be Clinton? She can't really be gone... just hurt. Why am I so alone?

"Are you okay? Can I get you anything?" a female officer asks, looking over at me.

Answers? My mother in law? My bed? A normal day?

"No thank you."

Other officers are laughing and joking in the background about their most recent parties. Foul language. Laughing as though my own world had not just been totally flipped upside down and hanging in some eternal limbo. They sound too real in this crazy dream I'm having. Nightmare rather. For a moment I am sad that this is so normal for them. Just another day on the job. But why us?

Suddenly I recognize the source of the gnawing emptiness inside me. I need God to step inside of this moment, wrap His tender arms around me, and feel present. Of course I know that He is. That He is not surprised by the way my morning is going. He's not disappointed that my brain is a wreck and that I'm desperately confused. I feel like a child who has wandered just beyond the sight of her parents. Beyond anyone familiar, with a crowd pushing and pulling her in different directions. The child looks up, can't see, and panics. Howls the familiar cry of terror that brings a mother or father running. Embraced. I need that embrace.

I know, regardless of what the chemicals in my brain can manage at this moment—the brain He designed—that He is here.

I also need to know that there are other people of faith around me: people who can understand this situation with me.

"Can we get a counselor or a pastor or someone?" I call out to the officer.

"Yes, you can call your pastor or we can get a chaplain out here once the detective has spoken with you."

Pastor Josh doesn't answer his phone. Of course not. This is a normal day for him. He is probably still sleeping or getting ready for our trip to El Sal. I set the phone down, feeling a little helpless, and stare at it through blurred vision. This time it's not because of missing contacts. I take a deep breath. Try to regain some semblance of composure.

"Is she dead?" I ask the officer.

This time the officer nods her head and says, "I believe so."

THE WEDDING BEFORE

WHEN I MET JEREMY, I was only twenty-one years old and he was twenty-eight years old. Our lives were filled with friendships and the beginning of careers. We met among a tight-knit group of friends from our mutual church. Not too long after meeting him, I moved in with four women from our friendship circle. Jeremy already lived in a house of guy-friends. Our group did everything together. And because of the nature of our constant interactions, shared meals, weekend trips, and living in community, many marriages came out of our friendship circle.

As most people have experienced, being in-love is not a magical wand for a conflict-free living. In fact, the passionate personalities of Jeremy and I led to many such conflicts. We were young, and in many ways, early in our journeys of learning what it meant to live out our faith beliefs. How to find our security in God and not the opinions of others. How to trust Him deeply with every circumstance, rather than lean on our insufficient abilities to succeed at this thing called "life." We had much to learn and committed to learn it together.

So after many break-ups and make-ups, Jeremy proposed to me. He stepped out of the fear that had held him back, and committed to break past patterns of using women and leaving them. Committed to sticking it out with me—a woman who intrigued him with her heart for the world, her many travels, her depth of insight into the Word of God, her green eyes. And her legs. He thinks I have gorgeous legs.

These legs would carry me many miles during the year of our engagement. To Canada, Guatemala, Paraguay, Brazil, Argentina. Meanwhile, he stayed in our hometown in California, preparing a home for his bride while I ministered abroad.

This was something that had drawn us together, a love for the world, cultures, and language. An African/Caribbean father and Danish/German mother had raised Jeremy, with his dark skin and curly black hair, between the countries of Colombia and the United States. I, on the other hand, was a freckled brunette with seven ear piercings, a nose piercing, and an eyebrow piercing. I had spent my childhood in California, but constantly moved from one place to the next. I had attended two preschools, two Kindergartens, two elementary schools, two junior highs, and almost two high schools. I made up for it by attending four Colleges/Universities. Both of us were wired for wandering. Discontent with a rooted life. We committed to spending life—marriage, child-rearing, retirement—on the cusps of new adventures and discoveries yet to be experienced around the world. And we were passionate for the things of God and sharing His love with whomever we met.

As was my style, I said, "Yes, I'll marry you!" then got on an airplane. An airplane that would have been one-way had he not proposed. But he did, thus making my one-way ticket a round-trip one, bringing me home three weeks before our wedding.

And so it went that Jeremy and I were married in July.

Medieval style.

Because who doesn't love a Medieval wedding?

We were anything but traditional.

And perhaps most parents would have balked at the idea of wearing costumes, sitting on stage with the couple, or being handed a sword or a crown as a prompt. Not our parents.

My dad, with Cherokee roots, displayed through a deep tan and bold cheekbones, proudly wore his rented King garb, with his head held high and proud. For a day, he was truly a king. My mom, her Italian-Choctaw features glowing, wore a beautiful handmade gown with a tiara snug in her black curly hair. Her hazel eyes only for her daughter.

Whatever she wanted. Because hadn't she at last found "the one?" She'd once consoled her oldest daughter with kind words and affirmation. "Don't worry, Marcy, one day you'll find the right man." To which I responded:

"Who's worried, mom?" with a shrug and a suspicious smile.

Today was the day.

My side of the family.

Jeremy's father, Clinton, had refused a costume for the day. It was far too... different. Besides, he still wasn't entirely convinced that Jeremy wasn't on drugs. Or that I wasn't pregnant. He was at least starting to believe that the latter may have been a false thought. Clinton, tall and dark-skinned with Caribbean flair, was 72 years old.

An islander of Colombia who had never planned on leaving all of his family, his culture, his sea for the likes of the United States. But a pregnant American wife on the verge of a nervous breakdown during civil riots in Colombia brought him to this land. And so he and his wife came to the U.S., where they taught as intellectual educators until he retired a couple of years prior. Retirement was spent in the garden and short visits to the island. He and this land tolerated each other rather well, but he had never quite found his tribe.

Now another opportunity arose again to return to his beloved Caribbean island for a visit. All of August was devoted to reunion with his people and his customs.

He refused to go.

A card from Mary Ann to Marcy:

I pray that you and Jeremy have a blessed and happy future. When the rough times come, and they will, let your faith be your support. Keep the lines of communication open if you can and repair them when they falter. I love you.

—Mary Ann.

We are getting married!

Mary Ann and Clinton at the wedding rehearsal.

Just want you to know that we are there for you in prayer and in spirit. I'm [a] cousin. I last saw [Clinton and Mary Ann] at the Family Reunion [on the island]... I know that what has happened is out or character for [Clinton]. What I see in the media is not my Cousin Clinton.

—*Clinton's Cousin*

A PERCEIVED THREAT

OUT OF THE BLUE, in the weeks leading up to our wedding, Clinton began to declare that he would not be going to Colombia on their summer vacation. He was adamant that there was a plot among his family members to kill him and steal his piece of land. His sister would use her witchcraft to murder her brother, or at the very least, to curse him, and he would not go and subject himself to that.

"They are crazy," he would say, "and I am not going." Mary Ann calmly assured him that his sister was not a witch and that his family had no plans to kill him. But as the day drew near, she began to wonder if she would be able to change his mind.

"Dad, this will be good for you," Jeremy said. "We promise, no one there wants to hurt you. They don't want to steal your land. They love you and are excited you're coming. Don't stay here in the hot summer and miss all the fun of spending time with your family." Clinton's irrational accusations about his family members were new to Mary Ann and their children. Though Clinton's personality had changed in small ways after his prostate cancer years ago, he had never been so outrightly disoriented amidst reality and his imagination. The family concerned themselves with it for the month or so that his rantings lasted until finally, something clicked, and Clinton changed his mind. He decided he would go after all. But he would not like it.

He preferred his garden.

A sort of surrogate to the life he'd known on the island. There he could make anything grow. And he could again live on the land and what it produced of his hard labor. Without any witches trying to steal his life. Or his land.

And at least the wedding was held outside, amidst a canvas of green foliage, climbing ivy, and acres of lush grass. He could almost feel comfortable here.

But not in a costume.

Until the morning of the wedding, that is. It was then, he decided, that to wear a suit would leave him the only "traditional" one in the wedding. And this would, naturally, make him stand out quite noticeably. Something he was not in favor of.

He preferred his wife's shadow. Gallantly. Lovingly. There was no other reason on the planet that he'd even be here, but for her. And she was worth it.

Only hours before the wedding, Clinton called. "Son," his Creole accent crackled over the phone, "I would like to wear a costume for your wedding today. Do you have one for me?"

No, his son did not, but as soon as the costume store opened, the two walked in with great purpose and limited time. And Clinton picked one out—black pants with a black vest, gold stitching down the front, with a long-sleeved white shirt beneath. He wore sunglasses and a black beret-style hat. With a dagger in his belt.

In this costume, Clinton's chest stood puffed a little more. His smile was contagious and charming as he escorted his wife around by hand, a sense of pride in his own beautiful bride and in this celebration of his son. Even if it completely lacked tradition—it was fun.

However, Jeremy's mom, Mary Ann, was perhaps the most visibly excited.

Clinton in his medieval costume for our wedding.

Mary Ann playfully blowing bubbles at my bridal shower.

Mary Ann's class changed my life. I was lucky enough to take Cultural Communities of CA and Linguistics from her. For the first time in a really time-consuming class, the effort I put into it reflected in my grade. She recognized my effort and praised me for it. Because of her I have decided that I don't want to live in a predominantly white upper-middle class neighborhood. I want to experience diversity, she made it seem interesting, fun, and a way to minister to others. I haven't read a newspaper article in the same way ever again. My favorite part about seeing her around campus was asking her how her can collecting was going. She was also approachable and easy to talk to about school or personal issues. I made a point to take a picture with her at my graduation. I will deeply miss her; the world will not be the same without her. My life will never be the same because of what she believed and taught.

—Former Student

THE HALLWAY TO TOMORROW

M<small>ARY</small> A<small>NN</small>'<small>S</small> only adornments at the wedding of her son were a small tiara fitted into her white hair and her token lopsided smile.

Mary Ann and Clinton in the wedding processional.

With these in their places, she giddily put on the blue Thai silk dress that a former student had gifted her. She had never fit in it before these last couple of months of long walks and weight-loss effort.

But being a woman who couldn't do only one thing, she turned her Weight Watcher's routine into a fundraiser as well. Dressed in a "trash-diving" sort of garb, laced with gloves, grocery bags, and an apron, Dr. Mary Ann Larsen-Pusey spent her early morning walks looking for cans, glasses, and bottles at the bottom of trash cans and dumpsters. These would be recycled in exchange for cash (which she did not really need but made the morning walk more productive). With the money she earned (or found) on these walks (and dives), Mary Ann purchased a flat-topped stove, a new computer, and butterflies for the wedding ceremony of Jeremy and Marcy. She also lost sixty pounds.

But this was not the only reason for her excitement that day. Mary Ann had watched her son trudge through a number of despairing relationships, one broken heart after another, either his own or the girl he'd left. She was quite vocal about—well, everything—but particularly the girls she approved of and the ones she did not. However, she tried to say it in a respectful, if not concerned, sort of way. She wanted her son's happiness.

Her own father's beliefs and opinions had been so loud and ferocious that he scared much of his family out of any relationship with him. And with his God. How Mary Ann longed to learn from that painful lesson. To pray quietly, hope silently, and walk alongside with carefully chosen words of advice and wisdom. Words that would not chase her children away from her if they disagreed. Or disfigure the reality of who God is, like her father's had done.

Not that she was afraid of an argument. Ha! Mary Ann loved a good debate. She was a highly esteemed professor at the local university. Her favorite courses to teach were the ones that deeply challenged and uprooted the entrenched stigmas, stereotypes, and cultural beliefs of her students. Not to prove them wrong and her right, but simply to get them thinking about life in ways they had never allowed themselves. Her courses were considered the hardest on campus.

"But not because of the load of course-work," she once explained to me. I'd attended the university where Mary Ann taught. However, I avoided Mary Ann's class at all costs, not wanting to take "the hardest class" on campus. I had no idea that I'd one day marry her son.

"My classes are the hardest because I make people think. I shake up what they think is true and ask them to consider the exceptions. To step outside of their box and acknowledge the bigger picture. This is the hard work." This made me regret not having taken one of Mary Ann's classes—I love a good discussion and thought-provoking topics.

Mary Ann's students either loved her classes or hated them. There wasn't a middle ground. But every student would say they left her classes somehow transformed. They couldn't think the same way anymore. No, too much of what they believed had been improved, in ways that led to more conscientious living, concern for others, generosity, a heart for the less fortunate. They left with a new freedom to love and engage others who are different, dividing walls in their hearts and minds torn down. And not just because she spoke it, but because they watched her live it, day in and day out.

I was so shocked to learn that the tragedy happened to your family. Mary Ann was one of the most inspiring and wonderful teachers that I have met in my life.
—Student of Mary Ann

She was helping me prepare to finish my last class before writing my thesis. I will miss her tremendously. Her understanding of the world really helped reshape my understanding for the better.
—Mentee of Mary Ann

Mary Ann had high expectations of her students but she was always available for encouragement. She was a willing source of information and an example of how knowledge and character join to produce an exceptional mentor. When I completed my Master's Degree she was more excited than myself. I, like so many others, will miss her.
—Student of Mary Ann

In fact, her last hours of life were spent counseling students by phone on their school projects, dropping off groceries on the doorstep of a struggling student, encouraging another student going through a life crisis. Yes, even her final hours were given over to others. To build them up. To make the world a better place by loving one person at a time. Intentionally. Thoughtfully. Sacrificially.

She had even offered to spend her lunch break driving Jeremy and me to the airport. We were leaving for a ten-day mission trip to El Salvador. She and Clinton had supported us financially. But she wanted us to know she supported us more deeply as well. How it made her heart happy to see her son using his bilingualism to serve and support others! To see his life radically changed from that of a lost and wandering addict to a focused and dedicated follower of their Savior, Jesus. How she had prayed fervently that he would find the truth on his own. How her heart had spent many years in quiet despair as he tasted one religion after another, one girl after another, and one addiction after another with an insatiable appetite. But nothing on this earth would fill it. She knew that. But she dared not say it. Lest she push him away as her own father had done to his children.

But we already had a ride to the airport. So she wished us well. Hugs. Blessings. And she walked down the dark hallway to the mother-in-law suite portion of the house. On the far end. Through doors. Down hallways.

If she had known this was a one-way trip, she might have stayed a bit longer. Hugged longer. Kissed foreheads. Held gazes. Given final words of love and hope and gratitude. Told me one more time how happy she was that Jeremy had married me and not any of the others. Told me one more time that there was no pressure to have a baby yet, but here's another cute blanket anyway. Ya know, for when you're ready. She might have gotten her son riled up in one final little debate or bit of dialogue, the kind that did not lead to angst, only engagement. Engagement with her cherished son. Because time is short and you never know when a "see you later" refers to the other side of Heaven's gates.

Letter from Mary Ann to Jeremy and me on our wedding:

We wish you the best that life can offer. May you grow together in harmony. When rough times come, lean on each other and ask the Almighty to sustain you. Remember that we love you and support you no matter what happens.

—Love, Mom and Dad

Mary Ann and Clinton hosted a family reunion the day after our wedding.

We did it!

IF YOU CAN KEEP A CAT ALIVE

Jeremy and I had watched the movie, How to Lose a Guy in Ten Days, in which one of the characters describes the order of life. First, get a plant and see if you can keep it alive. If it lives, get a pet and see if it stays alive. If it lives, then go ahead and try keeping children alive. Though the movie meant it in all humor, Jeremy and I saw some validity to this approach. Jeremy, a school teacher, and me, a counselor, were good candidates for keeping children alive. But it just made sense to try it out on plants and pets first.

The plants had thus far survived.

We began to look for something small that could withstand apartment life.

Cats.

We found two kittens in the newspaper in need of a home. I called the number and learned that the owners of these two kittens were moving out of state and couldn't take their little pets. They hoped the two kittens could stay together, as one of them was more skittish than the other and relied quite a bit on her brother to determine if the world was safe.

Jeremy and I decided to try them out.

A couple days later, a woman showed up with two cat carriers in tow, containing Guy and Staci. I led her to our bedroom, which also had quick access to a bathroom. I sat on the floor beside the cages, leaning my back against the bed. Jeremy stood in the doorway while the woman got situated between the bed and the bathroom. The woman, also a vet, opened the doors to the cages while speaking very softly and tenderly. She explained to the us that, while only five months old, the kittens would need some tender loving care and reassurance that they were safe.

A sweet little grey striped tabby poked his head out from the cage. He looked around the room with big eyes, taking in each person, the bed, the cage, even the decorations on the wall. He casually sniffed the lining of the cage door as if there was nothing at all unusual about his situation. He let out a soft mew before cautiously stepping his front two paws out of the cage door. The vet reached down to pet his head, scooping him up before he could make another decision about his new home. She stroked his soft fur while giving him a quick shot in the back of his neck. The tabby didn't even seem to notice as a light purr escaped from him. With eyes barely open, he feigned nonchalance about this place. I reached out to pet him carefully, crooning at how cute and sweet he was.

"He is a little bigger than I expected. How old are they again?" I asked.

"About five months old." I thought about that and realized kittens grow quite a bit in five months. But even so, this first one seemed really sweet so far.

"Jeremy, doesn't he make you think of a Tommy Lee?" I asked.

Jeremy giggled, "Yeah, he does! Let's name him that. Tommy Lee Guy. But we can just call him Tommy."

"Tommy," I repeated. Yes, it suited him well. The vet set him down gently. Tommy looked up at us and meowed again. I stroked his head and smiled. Very casually, Tommy walked to the edge of the bed, then under it. "Hmmmm," I said. "That could be interesting. Think he'll come out?"

Tommy

The vet smiled and nodded, her sandy blond hair pulled back from her face. "Yeah, when he feels safe, he'll come out exploring," she said. "This one, however, is a little bit more challenging. She is also very sweet but easily scared and distrustful. With some time and love, she will come around."

The small one had yet to peek out of her opened-door cage. The vet leaned down and peeked in, talking softly to the little creature huddled in the back corner. Eyes glowed from the fugitive of the cage's darkness. "Come on sweetie, it's okay," soothed the vet. The eyes continued to glow. The vet carefully reached in and grabbed the neck of Tommy's sister, forcing her out of her darkness and into the bright world of her new home. The vet quickly pulled her into a comfortable position in her arms.

This kitten was gorgeous.

Creamy white fur with a soft gray mask set on her face, enhancing her deep blue eyes. "Oh wow," I said. We took in her small frame while the vet injected the kitten with a shot. The kitten's ears were flat— clearly she was only tolerating this current inconvenience.

"She looks a little like a spider monkey," I remarked. It was true. The way the gray lines framed her white face gave her the cute look of the famous monkey, yet somehow with her creamy coat, only served to enhance her beauty. "Let's call her Mona."

Jeremy immediately agreed. There didn't seem to be a more fitting name for her than the Spanish word for "female monkey."

Mona

Mona was set down gently, but before it even appeared that her feet had touched the ground, she was under the bed. "Well, welcome home Tommy and Mona," said Jeremy, while I peered under the bed after two pairs of glowing eyes.

"I guess we just go on with our day as normal and see if our new guests ever care to join us."

And of course, in time, they both came out from under the bed. Tommy was the first to check out the full potential of the apartment. He jumped on everything worth jumping on, sniffed out every corner, and sought out a food dish and water bowl. Mona came out much later, when the apartment was very quiet and Jeremy and I were getting ready for bed. Like a small phantom, she skittered along walls, floated in and out of rooms, and caused food and water to vanish without the smallest sign of her presence otherwise. Tommy, on the other hand, was sold out and all for making the best of his new home. He rubbed against legs, purred like there was no tomorrow, and found a lap as good a napping spot as any.

Tommy and Mona.

In time, Mona came around as well. Her progress was slow, but she began to nap in public places and found refuge under the bed less and less. She found a place for her sweet, feminine meow among the loud and clear call of her brother. And she would totally lose herself in a chase for the light of a laser. With lots of work and love, Tommy and Mona found their places in the small home of Jeremy and I. We had no idea how short our time with them would be.

Brother and sister all snuggled together.

BUY A HOUSE?

"Buy a house?" I asked incredulously. "Why in the world do we need to buy a house? We're not going to live anywhere long enough to... buy a house!"

Jeremy's suggestion wasn't going over too well.

"Because every month that we pay rent on this apartment, we're just throwing money away. Why not invest in something? Put our money toward something that is ours."

"But—buy a house?" I felt like my newly-wedded world was crumbling at the edges. We did not need a house. True, it was not the most ideal of living situations. But we were together. What else mattered? And what about living around the world? We had only been married about six months. I had spent most of that time looking for a job, which I had now successfully obtained. A house? Wouldn't that seal my fate forever? Keep me tied down to this town, like a tetherball to a pole, when my true longing was to live, well, everywhere?

Our original, premarital plan had been to pay off our school loans and then travel the world for a year. Decide where we wanted to live and find ways of serving there. Already we were taking a trip to El Salvador with our church as co-leaders. Then immediately after that we would fly to Paraguay on a vision-casting trip with one of our pastors. To dream, plan, discuss ways of staying involved with the people I had grown to love during my year of life there.

The plan appeared to be crumbling.

It could also be that my parents had never bought a house. Not because of philosophy or the cause of nomadism, we just couldn't afford it. Wealthy people buy houses, not newly-married world wanderers.

But I loved him. And I understood that marriage was a team. As a new wife, I was learning that God was to be the head of our household, and Jeremy the head of our marriage, and though discussion, argument, and opinion-sharing were all a part of "team life"—ultimately, I would respect his decision and follow him. I would also be his greatest prayer warrior and support. Entrusting this new life to a fallible human trying to follow the guidance of Jesus was not easy. For either of us. But unconditional love and respect is never easy if you haven't first experienced such yourself. Fortunately, Jeremy and I were students of such love and respect under the direction of God's Word, His presence in our lives, and a healthy, thriving church community around us.

Besides, he was really intelligent. He'd been raised upper-middle class. He knew how to use a fork and a knife correctly (which he'd quickly taught me upon watching my more barbaric attempts at eating). He was wise with money, even if he didn't keep a check register. He had been a bachelor with a teaching career. There was always enough money.

But aside from his classier upbringing, he really did have a good head on his shoulders. He had experienced a lot of life in his short twenty-nine years and had wisely learned from his observations. If I ever wondered about one of life's mysteries, Jeremy was one of the few who could explain it. He was solid in character as well as in build. He deeply valued integrity and depth in his relationships. His word was as good as any signed deed. I knew to trust his counsel.

But that is not what finally convinced me to buy a house.

THE COCKROACH TOWN HALL

TOMMY AND MONA were not our only new guests.

Their tannish-brown bodies crept and crawled in every unsuspecting place. Little darkness-starved creatures making their homes and hide-outs in any shoe, closet, cupboard. Any dark place long enough for them to sniff it out and sneak right in.

That is the problem with apartment living.

A note on the door had stated:

On Friday, Peter's Pest Control will be spraying each of the apartments for cockroaches. If you would like to be included, please let the apartment office know. You will need to remove every item from your kitchen. Thank you.

—Apartment Management

Well, we did not have a cockroach problem and removing every item from the kitchen did not sound like the newly-wedded kind of bliss promised by Hollywood and every romance novel. So we opted out.

The thing is, cockroaches are clever in the ways their insignificant little brains can manage. And they seem to be made out of some kind of insect-iron. You can slam them with a shoe, and their shape seems to pop back into cockroach-form and off they go. Unscathed.

Or spray them with Raid. And spray and spray and spray until they drown in Raid's chemical foam of death. Spray just a little and they seem to delight in the slip and slide you've created for them, like toddlers at a waterpark.

In the instance of apartment living, the cockroaches of Sequoia Ridge Apartments held a public town-hall for all creatures on death-row.

"Listen up... Peter's Pest is coming on Friday. Apartments 1A through 215B are all getting sprayed—but not apartment 241B. Who is in favor of relocating to apartment 241B? For the sake of all future roaches? Aye-Aye!"

And they packed up their little roachy bags, said their final good-byes to all of their favorite nooks and crannies in the other apartments, and made their way to our place.

To my horror.

Friday came and went, ushering in a flood of refugee roaches. They climbed the walls and ceilings, threatening to skydive on any given whim. Even Tommy and Mona began to paw at the critters less and less as they became a part of the everyday scenery.

But when one climbed up my leg—as I sat cowering on the couch, counting the crunchy creatures overwhelming my home—I'd had enough.

"I have lived in developing countries that did not have as many cockroaches crawling as this! I want to move!" I sobbed, kicking my leg into the air reflexively, sending one of the creepy crawlers through the air.

And so it was that Jeremy and I began our house hunt. Not because of the wisdom of financial stewardship, but to escape the onslaught of lessons learned in apartment living, if you do not get your cockroach-free apartment sprayed by Peter's Pest, expect to be the next hotel manager for every escaped cockroach convict.

Boxes could not be packed fast enough, raided quickly enough, and loaded on a truck bound anywhere with enough speed to satisfy the new desire that I had to vacate this "lover's den" of ours.

Yet had we known that Mary Ann would be murdered in our new home in two month's time, we might have just made do with our new houseguests.

MOVING IN WITH THE IN-LAWS

"WE'D LIKE you to consider buying our house," stated Mary Ann, a twinkle in her eye. This was a beautifully thought out scheme of hers. "If you buy our house, we could move all of our stuff into the mother-in-law suite and you could live in the rest of the house. Then, when we come back from Colombia for visits, we have a place to stay and store our things." This was a sure-fire plan. Mary Ann and Clinton would have free storage and vacation housing, Jeremy and I would have a house.

I sighed. If I have to buy a house, I kind of wanted to get to pick it. I glanced at Jeremy. He nodded quietly as his mother's plan weaved its way through the logical centers of his brain. I looked around the living room. The living room that would soon be mine—sorta.

"What we'll do is add you two to the title of the house so that we are all four on it. Then, you two can refinance the loan into your names, with an additional $200,000 to pay us for the house. That will save you quite a bit in taxes. It's a gift."

It was a gift. A beautiful gift. The kind of gift that lots of young couples get excited about. A four bedroom house in the main portion, with two bathrooms, a den, a living room, a formal dining room and kitchen. The home was set on a huge lot in a cul-de-sac with a well-cultivated garden (thanks to Clinton) in the same part of town that Jeremy and I loved living in. In addition, the home had a mother-in-law suite with another master bedroom, living room, and bathroom. Along with a shared laundry room. It was huge.

But it was not my choice.

This was not the way I had envisioned my life going.

Had I ever envisioned buying a house, it would have involved a house-search, surveying all of the available treasures of homes available and picking one that spoke to my inner little girl. The one who played "house" all my years growing up, creating homes with rope, sheets, and clothespins in the garage.

This house was much better than sheets and line, but it was not even among options. And what would it be like to live with my in-laws? They said they planned on moving in October. That would be three months sharing a space with the parents. I loved them, but could I live with them?

My mind flashed back to the cockroach that had made its way up my leg a couple nights before. My in-laws were a way better option than those fiends.

"Let's do it."

THE MOVE

THE MOVE WENT RELATIVELY WELL. Many of our friends showed up to help cart our boxed-up lives the one-mile trek to our new home. But not without "Raiding" each box first—just to make sure none of the little critters relocated with us.

Boxes were dropped off in the various empty bedrooms of the main portion of the house. Jeremy and I were certainly in for an upgrade from our first ten months of marriage. We now had a large master bedroom, an entire room for an office, and a guest room. Plus an extra bathroom with a huge bathtub. And way more living room and den space then we could imagine using. Mary Ann's lopsided smile was as wide as it could be. Clinton sat in his rocking chair in front of the television, watching his favorite show, pausing from his entertainment to cast greetings of "hello" to friends passing through. Tommy and Mona were released from the arms of their masters and began to roam their new spacious home. Tommy as carefree as ever and Mona with her usual trepidation.

Not all of Mary Ann and Clinton's belongings had been moved to the back rooms yet. "We'll move that back as we are able," Mary Ann had told us. And she was true to her word. From that moment until her last, Mary Ann was packing, moving, reorganizing her American life into a one-bedroom mother-in-law suite.

Having been the child of the depression era, Mary Ann kept fifteen of every item. Toothbrushes, toothpaste, tomato sauce, tablecloths, detergent—if it was on sale, it was good enough to buy five of them, just in case. It was three years after Mary Ann's death before Jeremy or I had to buy a new toothbrush because of the stockpile we'd inherited from his mom.

Going through the food pantry, however, was Mary Ann's most difficult challenge. In it she had kept the jams her own mother had made. Her mother had been gone for seven years. "I know this probably seems strange," Mary Ann said, "but I have held onto these ever since she passed away." Her eyes blinked back tears of nostalgia as she held a jar of strawberry jelly tenderly in her hand. "It has been a constant reminder of her." I sat uncomfortably at the dining room table. My discomfort was not due to seven-year-old jars of jelly. That seemed sentimental and touching. It was not Mary Ann's tears. They were appropriate for a woman who had loved her mother and grieved to see her go.

It was the lack of life experience to relate.

"I've never lost someone really close to me." I picked at my fingernails. "Not that I want to lose anyone, I just think I've been fortunate in that way. But someday, someone will die and I don't like that idea." Mary Ann smiled a soft smile. Grief over the loss of loved ones was not unfamiliar to her. It was a bittersweet part of life, to love and lose.

"Well, my mom is living free of all her pain with Jesus now, and I know I will see her again. That is a hope I hang on to—that this life is not the end—just a passing breath until eternity presses in and ushers us into forever, together. As for these jellies—well, they are not coming. It's time to throw them out, I think." She tossed the tokens of her treasured memories into the trash bin.

Little did she know that her reunion with her mother was scheduled for a couple of weeks later, on the other side of Heaven's gates. She would not be taking jelly, or any other memento from her time on earth, only her soul and the seal that marked her as one of God's own.

Welcomed by the embraces of her Heavenly Father and her earthly mother, and the others who had journeyed the path from the grave to the spiritual realm and found healing and freedom.

A freedom that would not belong to her husband for quite some time.

THE STOLEN LICENSE PLATE

"Jeremy," called Clinton, as we made our way out of the front door. "I have your license plate. I was afraid someone was going to steal it so I took it off for you to keep it safe."

Jeremy and I glanced at each other.

"Uh, thanks dad," said Jeremy, stepping forward to retrieve the license plate from his dad.

We stepped out of the door in the kind of strange silence that speaks multitudes. Our car appeared as though someone had vandalized it of its plate—and indeed, someone had. In the hopes of keeping others from doing the same.

"Jeremy, your dad is getting older..." I let my sentence trail off. How do you tell someone that his or her dad might need some help?

"Yeah, I've noticed some things too."

One day, Clinton had become overwhelmed with the fear of burglars who might come and rob his home of his prized possessions, whatever they were. In his paranoia, he grabbed every plastic bin in the house that he could find and built a wall. This plastic bin barrier was supposed to keep burglars away. At some point, Clinton decided that his wall was insufficient or placed wrongly, and he tossed them over the fence into his neighbor's yard.

"Your husband threw these bins into my yard," stated the neighbor to Mary Ann when he returned them. She thanked him, closed the door, and stored these things up in her heart.

"Clinton has done some strange things," she told me in a hushed voice over the phone. "Because I don't want to embarrass or shame him, I don't really have anyone to talk to about this," she said, trailing off into tidbits of Clinton's odd behavior, none of it violent, just unusual. Before I could say much in response or ask questions, Mary Ann said that she needed to get going. And never mentioned it again.

On a different day, Clinton got into a heated debate with Mary Ann over her weight loss.

"You are having an affair with our gardener, I know it!"

But she was not.

Her response was calm but confident. "I am losing weight for my own health, not for anyone else. Not for the gardener or any other man but you. I love you and I am not having an affair."

It was June and Jeremy had the summer off of work as a schoolteacher. This led to a lot of time spent in the garden with his dad. And in conversations with his parents.

Including the conversation about all of the "missing" money that Mary Ann must be hiding for some mysterious purpose. The three of them sat at the table in the living room of the mother-in-law suite. Someone had had enough of Clinton's accusations around money and decided to pull it all out and look over it together. Bank statements, receipts, and IRA documents littered the table. Organizational bins and filing drawers surrounded the crew. Jeremy acted as mediator between the accuser and the accused.

"I just know you have millions of dollars that you are hiding away for some reason," said Clinton.

So the numbers were mapped out, bank accounts reviewed, explanations given.

Not a penny was missing.

Even with all of the evidence clearly pointing to Mary Ann's innocence, Clinton was still sure that she was hiding money and having affairs.

Later, when Jeremy was sorting through the paperwork of Clinton and Mary Ann, only weeks after her death, he found a note with Mary Ann's script: A list of psychiatrists and their phone numbers.

So she had known.

She had acknowledged that Clinton was not his usual, charming, loving self and needed some help.

But that is as far as she got.

A list, a haunting list, to show that she knew something was up, but not in enough time to stop just that from killing her.

Paper found with Mary Ann's Handwriting after her death (with corrections made in Clinton's handwriting):

Tell Dr. Unhle:

    Sleeplessness for several weeks.

    Odd behavior – seeing things.

    Talk of death- fear of being killed or arrested.

    Changed mind about going to Colombia – insists his health is not up to it.

    Has barricaded doors at night.

    Removed clothes from two storage bins and threw lids in neighbor's backyard – then called 911 to say someone broke in and did it.

    Won't go to his family's reunion because "everyone is out to get him."

WRONG (He underlined the above portion of her note (which he had apparently found) and wrote "wrong" and circled it beneath her list.

I WON'T SIGN WITHOUT HIM

JEREMY and I were added to the title of the house. Now all that was needed was the signing of the loan documents in order to take over the loan.

Jeremy, Clinton, Mary Ann, and I all sat around the large round dining room table with the loan broker. Mary Ann led the conversation, orchestrating all of the details of the transaction she had dreamed up. The others were quiet as the loan broker flipped through the mini-book of pages to be signed, explaining this section of fine-print, numbers, numbers, and more numbers.

"You will sign here and sign there."

Mary Ann alone raised questions for clarification.

I sat quietly in my chair. This is it. We are buying a house. Not just any house. Their house. The moment and all it encompassed oozed through my body, mingling with the blood that kept my brain thinking and my heart beating. I mindlessly fingered the pen in front of me, ready to do my duty of signing beside all of the "x"s. Will they finally move their stuff to their rooms when we are paying the bill? A month had passed and there were still many signs of Mary Ann and Clinton in the main portion of the house. Moving can be terribly slow when you have not thrown a thing away since the depression ended.

Or when you save every jar your deceased mother canned seven years prior.

Or when saying goodbye is really hard—but fast approaching.

I tried to be understanding and patient. Will this ever feel like home?

Mary Ann's question brought me back to the paperwork. "Where is Clinton's name on these documents?"

"We only needed one of your names," the broker responded.

Mary Ann's lips twitched. She sat up, quite resolutely. "We are not signing any documents that do not include Clinton's name."

"It is really not necessary, Mrs. Pusey. This paperwork is quite sufficient—"

"I am not signing any documents that do not acknowledge Clinton. These will need to be reprinted. He and I are in this transaction together."

The loan broker, defeated, shuffled her papers together. With a smile plastered to her face, she said she would get the documents corrected and would reschedule.

"Thank you," Mary Ann said, walking her to the door. This decision did not surprise Jeremy or me. Mary Ann was intentional about respecting her husband and his wishes. Clinton himself had not said much about his absent name. Nor would he. He did not need to. Mary Ann was looking out for both of them.

Mary Ann loved her husband dearly. She loved his South American heritage, their common love for language and people, the freedom he had given her to become the woman she was. Always by her side, cheering her on. Sacrifice after sacrifice had been laid down so she could take a break from the stress the Colombian civil unrest was causing her, attain her PhD, and flourish as an educator. They had spent a number of years geographically separated while visa issues detained Clinton, and securing a good education propelled Mary Ann into another world.

And though she regretted some of the mistakes she had made at that time, she could see how blessed she was to have a man such as Clinton at her side.

He was a faithful letter-writer.

Every week of their separations, he wrote to fill her in on life in Colombia, how the kids were doing (when he had them) and how much he missed her. She cherished those letters and saved every one.

The least she could do, now, was make sure his name was on the loan documents. A way to show him, over and over, how much she respected him and the life he had allowed her. That she would not forget who her life partner was, no matter how difficult things could be.

Even when he accused her of affairs.

Or of stealing money.

Or built barricades of protection with bins.

For better or for worse... she was his. And she loved him.

The loan could wait if it spoke, "I respect you, husband."

Besides, there was plenty of time... right?

FATEFUL FRIEND

FAITH ARRIVED.

She was a friend of Mary Ann's from many years back. She was slightly taller than Mary Ann (as quite a few were) and moved with grace and ease, as though gliding through a room. Her smile was warm and friendly and it was easy to see why she and Mary Ann were close. The kind of friends for whom many years can pass… but the moments spent together are as though time has stood still and distance has never been further than a hug.

She stayed a few days in our home, devoted entirely to investing in her friendships with Clinton and Mary Ann. Both women wanted to capture the moments forever through the lenses of their cameras, knowing that time was short and who knew how long until the next visit? A pictorial memory.

It is because of the love these two women had for each other, and their cameras, that Jeremy and I have the last photo taken of Mary Ann.

Mary Ann sits in her retirement gift—a rocking chair from the university with an inscription. Her leg casually crosses the other, her arms relaxed on the arms of the chair. She smiles her famous smile, one eye slightly closed, one corner of her mouth slightly turned down. Her white hair stands out against the mahogany brown of the chair.

She is perfectly framed in the photo.

Her last photo.

It's her smile and that gleam that one notices, the way even a camera could capture that look—the look that says something humors her but what it is will remain her secret. Her own personal joke. Life humored her, though not in a mocking, condescending way. She simply found joy in being. In empowering others to make the world a better place.

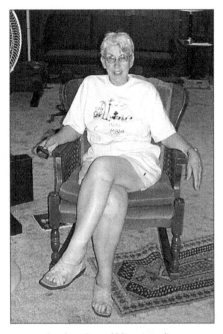

Our last photo of Mary Ann alive.

*S*he laughed easily. Mostly at herself. But a good twist of words, stroke of insight, or a bit of irony could do the trick as well.

Faith found no shortage of laughter during her visit.

But something stood out to her nonetheless.

Days after she returned to her own home, she phoned Mary Ann.

This time there was no laughter.

"Mary Ann... in my time with you, I noticed that Clinton seemed... off. Have you considered getting some help for him?"

Mary Ann sighed. "Yes, I know... but I just cannot bring myself to admit it. I really do not have anyone to talk to about it because I do not want to embarrass him. But you are right, things have been strange." Mary Ann did not elaborate on all of the strange things that Clinton was doing, but there were many. She stored up these incidents in her heart and in her mind, knowing the day was fast approaching when she would need to end her denial and look into help for him. Had they grown "old" already?

She pulled out a pen, paper, and the phone book.

I was really impressed by her interest in the persons she met, the quality of her attention, her curiosity, her sensibility. She was so open-minded, so clear in her political options, that I was astonished to find a "gringa" so compromised with those rejected by the political, ideological and economical systems... I want to give to you this testimony of the memory of [Mary Ann], and of how she marked the lives of everyone she knew as a fairy godmother capable of opening our eyes to the grief of those who reject the other, or accept discrimination, without being able to recognize it nor fight against it.

—Colombian Colleague

OUR FIRST AND LAST ANNIVERSARY

OUR FIRST ANNIVERSARY was in a week.

"We know it's a little early, but we wanted to spend some time with you today and give you a gift," said Mary Ann. She smiled with that delightful gleam in her eyes. The gleam that let others in on a little secret—she was enjoying the moment. That gleam and half smile were a favored expression of many of her friends and family. Usually, only moments later, erupted a laugh that shook the heavens and everything in between. That laugh was felt deeply and genuinely and never passed unnoticed. Today was no different.

After a nice homemade Colombian-style lunch, we retreated to the living room. Clinton took his place in the rocker, Mary Ann in the opposite chair. I sat at their feet on the carpet with Jeremy right beside me.

There was that gleam again.

Mary Ann pulled a rolling cooler from behind her and presented it to the us. Its blue lid shined that new-plastic glaze look. The white handle ended with a red bow.

A typical gift from Mary Ann—very practical and unwrapped. The bow was an exception.

Regardless of the practicality and lack of décor, Jeremy and I welcomed the gift.

"Is this because we always borrow your cooler?" I asked, teasing.

Seemingly a little bashful (which was unusual for Mary Ann), she said, "No! I just felt bad that when you did borrow ours, it was in such awful condition! So this is our gift—to many future camping trips and picnics." It really was a gift that we could use. We expressed our gratitude with hugs and kisses and genuine "Thanks!"

Each one of us shared a highlight from the last year. "I have loved sharing Sunday breakfasts with you two, and have really missed it when we have had to reschedule," said Mary Ann, smiling. Nearly every Sunday since our wedding day, Jeremy and I had driven the one mile to their house. A delicious breakfast of quiche, sausage, fresh-squeezed orange juice, and biscuits greeted us each week. Conversations taken for granted. Meals that passed too quickly. Valuable time... limited time spent together each week. It was a highlight for each of us.

Mary Ann then took a more serious expression. "Jeremy, I am so glad that you married Marcy. I have been praying for a long time for the wife you would choose. I am so, so happy it is Marcy. Marcy, you balance him and us. Thank you for loving our son." Teary eyes looked from one to another. These were words to be stored up. A mother-in-law expressing gratitude for her daughter-in-law. Jeremy smiled and hugged me.

Clinton was not to be out-done. This man of few words spoke up with eloquence and said, "Son, I have never seen you so happy in your whole life. I am glad, also, that you married Marcy. She is now my daughter and I love her like my own. Marrying her was the best decision you ever made. I am proud of you, son. Happy anniversary you two." Oh how it does a son's heart proud to hear his parents speak of his bride in this way! We all four knew that this moment was precious, a sort of rare opportunity to say the things you want to say, things that normally stay hidden in thoughts or spoken at eulogies. Things you think, Why didn't I say that when they were alive and could appreciate it?

But on this day, those silent thoughts became intentional gifts. One could never wonder if Mary Ann or Clinton enjoyed the young family blooming and growing beneath their wings. They had spoken their hearts freely.

And what a gift it was.

Because seven days later, on the first anniversary of this son and his bride, Mary Ann was dead. Her husband in custody. And life was upside down.

There would be no more Sunday morning breakfasts of quiche and fresh-squeezed orange juice from the tree outside.

No more opportunities to say the words that thoughts harbor.

No more hugs, kisses, affirmations.

Only a sense that life had been truly robbed of a gem. An anniversary of a wedded union now marking the anniversary of a life taken too soon. Every day, forever, this anniversary of grief would come four days before the anniversary of joy.

Letter to Jeremy and I from Mary Ann and Clinton for our first anniversary:

This note is to let you know how much we desire the best for you and to congratulate you on your upcoming anniversary. We know you love each other and are working at building a strong relationship. May God bless you on your upcoming trip and give you all that you desire and need.

—Mom & Dad

*The last photo of Mary Ann and Clinton together, about a week
before our first anniversary.*

FAX MACHINES AND DANGER SIGNS

Ooh, I can fax it! I thought as I shuffled through the final forms I needed for our trip to El Salvador. The only fax machine was in the mother-in-law suite of Mary Ann and Clinton. I walked down the long hallway from my room to the kitchen. Clinton stood over the counter cooking fish. How he loved fish! It took him back to his home on the island where fisherman, each morning, climb into their small boats and cast their nets. Some even dive in with their nets and swim after the fish. Red Snapper, coconut rice, and plantains were the reward for the successful fisherman. And oh, how that fresh-caught fish tasted better than any fish he could find here in the States.

But it would do. He poured himself into coaxing the flavor of the fish to mingle with his spices and lemon.

"Clinton, do you mind if I use your fax machine? I just have one form to send off," I inquired.

Clinton turned to me, his face filled with emotion. "Marcy, you are my daughter-in-law. I love you like my own daughter. Everything I have is yours, everything!" he gushed.

Not that Clinton was not kind, he was. But this was a bit over the top, even for him. I had noticed that in the last couple of days, Clinton had been above and beyond kind. Gushing over every little sentiment and opportunity to express it. *Sheesh, aging suits him well,* I thought, as I headed down another hallway toward Clinton's living area.

I walked into their large living area, passed the table beside the door, the couch, and the television, to the far back wall. The fax sat on a shelf beside the large open window overlooking Clinton's beautiful garden. His natural art made a masterpiece framed by a windowsill, filling the room with shades of green and budding life. Lettuce, tomatoes, strawberries, squash all lined up in perfect rows, separated by stepping stones. Though I did not have one ounce of skill with gardens, I truly appreciated the beauty of Clinton's work. Years of composting, flipping soil, and caring for each and every growing thing had made a fertile crescent in our own backyard.

I inserted the paper into the fax machine, punched the phone number, and waited.

Clinton entered the room quietly behind me, rummaging through papers on the counter beside the door to the room. To one end of the counter was a door leading outside—a private entry for this portion of the house. The other end of the counter found a door leading to their master bedroom, laundry room, bathroom, and eventually mine and Jeremy's portion of the house.

As the dial tone of the fax echoed through the room, the hair on the back of my neck stood straight up. The feeling that I was being watched brought tingles from my head to my toes. *Of course I'm being watched, silly,* I thought to myself, *I am in their living room and he is in here.* I began to experience waves of "Danger! Danger! Danger!" throughout my nervous system, speeding up the pace of my heart, breaking me into a cold sweat. *What in the world is going on?* I thought to myself, ashamed.

Clinton was one of the most gentle, loving people I knew. I had never seen him raise his arm against anything, let alone raise his voice. Even in his accusations toward Mary Ann, on bad days, he was very calm and collected. Even now he shuffled along the back of the room, working on whatever it was he had been doing.

Still, I could not break myself from the feeling that I was in danger. Still feeling ashamed, I turned to face him while the fax printed across town somewhere, feeling safer with my back to the machine than toward this kind, aging father-in-law. My breathing slowed, my heart returned to normal, and my brain slowed the message to a normal thought-stream—though it stayed alert.

Clinton didn't even seem to notice the conflict going on within me. He simply carried on whatever activity he was doing, seemingly oblivious to me standing in the room.

The fax could not send fast enough.

As soon as the confirmation printed, I said, "Thank you, Clinton," and left the room quickly (but not so quickly as to appear uncomfortable, and offend my father-in-law.)

Two days later, this very moment jolted back into my awareness.

I sat, leaning against my friend's wall, a haven from the media, concerned friends, her best friends. A place to lower my head and bawl at the injustice of Mary Ann's death. At the way my world—my ordinary world—with jobs, houses, friends, church, mission trips, was flipped on its head. And she was gone. And he was in jail. And I could not go home.

Home.

To where Mary Ann's blood still seeped into concrete.

Where it speckled the walls.

Where I had slept peacefully, believing that all was well in the world and I was safe.

While Mary Ann was being murdered in the other end of our home, feet away from where I'd stood with the fax machine.

Bedroom door wide open.

An invitation to a murderer, to come and find my sleeping body and do with it what he would while I slumbered.

Yet somehow I had been spared. Somehow between killing his wife and walking down two hallways, Clinton snapped out of it. Snapped out of it enough to call 9-1-1 for help and waken his sleeping children.

That is when it shook me out of my thoughts.

The memory. The fax machine, his abundant kindness, and my chilling fear when my back was to him.

Was that a warning? Was my spirit sensitive to the darkness that was about to unveil itself in reality? Could I have heard more clearly and stopped this grief? No, the warning was not that clear.

But how strange. I will always wonder about that moment, the moment of what seemed to be irrational fear, proven to be quite rational.

We have fond memories of Mary Ann. Her dedication to her students, speaking out against injustice, willingness to serve others, and the ability to laugh at herself speak volumes about her character. We mourn her loss.

—Former Colleagues

MISSED MOMENTS AND FINAL GOODBYES

IT WAS ALMOST time to go.

The next day, Jeremy and I were getting on a plane with our church. We'd planned on spending ten days in El Salvador, co-leading a team with our Associate Pastor, Josh. Then another week in Paraguay to plan for teams to come the following year. We had spent week after week preparing with our church team. We wrote letters. Raised funds. Bought plane tickets. I was excited to return to my "family" in Paraguay, to reconnect with friendships I had spent almost a year with during my engagement to Jeremy. Excited to introduce them to the man they had heard plenty about.

Our bags were packed and it was nearly time for bed. Jeremy was across the hall in the office. I was in our bedroom. There was tension in the air. Perhaps the tension that surrounds most young-marrieds when they live with the parents. Or when they try to pack for two weeks together and have different opinions about how and what to pack. Or perhaps the tension was simply related to two passionate people, two rivers, converging into one, where the rapids froth and foam in a torrent, until they ease a way down the crevices and reach a harmony within itself.

We two, almost one year in, were still in the throes of finding harmony and balance in the collision of our two rivers. Perhaps this is the tension that hovered over us that night. Whatever it was, Jeremy was in one room. I was in the other.

Mary Ann came down the hallway. "Hello? Are you guys here?" Jeremy answered from the office. She stepped in and they chatted for a bit. He was a bit distracted as he moved around the office.

"Do you guys need a ride to the airport tomorrow?" I heard her ask. I called from the other room that we already had a ride, but thank you very much. She stood making small chat for a few more minutes. "Well, if something changes, let me know. I do not mind taking you."

"Thanks, Mom," Jeremy said, giving her a quick smile. "Do you mind feeding Tommy and Mona while we are gone?"

"Sure, that's no problem." She turned to walk down the hallway.

"Take care!" she called out, as she faded into the darkness.

The darkness that would never return her. Our memories of her forever end with this moment. A moment taken for granted because it was not supposed to end like this. In this way. With her walking down a dark hallway forever.

"Why didn't I hug her?" Jeremy later cried out. "Did she know I loved her?" Jeremy and I would hold each other and weep over what was our final goodbye. So insignificant. So normal. Without any respect for life's ends and beginnings. Without any suspicion that what life seems to be at this moment, may not hold true in the next. Regretting the tension of two rivers, the stress of packing bags for cross-continental travel, and our self-focus that kept us from seeing more. From knowing more.

From stopping her.

From saying, "NO! Do not go down that hallway! Stay with us. Let's just... be. Together. You and us. For as long as we have."

Instead, she walked, and we let her, not knowing that her life had only a few hours left in its earthly clock. The hallway was not the end for her, but it was the end for us. The way we would remember our final interaction with such a precious soul. So casual. Forgetting, in the midst of all that sought our attention, that she was worth setting it down, giving a hug, and saying, "I love you."

And she was more than worth it.

But all the same, she walks off into the darkness of the hallway and does not return.

I lived with [Mary Ann and Clinton] for a year and never knew nothing but kindness from the both of them. Clinton and Mary Ann were very kind to open their home to me and my family when they came to visit. I loved both Clinton and Mary Ann. I talk to my family often about them because they truly did leave a lasting impression of hospitality and kindness to all that stayed in their home.

—Former Student and Housemate

HOW TO DIE WELL

IT HAS ONLY BEEN PIECED TOGETHER, in small snippets, what Mary Ann did with her last few hours, after coming out of the darkness of the hallway into the light of her portion of the house. Perhaps her husband greeted her. Asked how the kids were. Were they ready for their trip? Maybe it would be nice to have the house to themselves for a bit. Or maybe it would just be too quiet. Like being empty nesters all over again.

She spent the next number of hours chatting with students on the phone, encouraging them in their life and educational goals and current class projects. She listened. Her undivided attention for those who needed it, for however long they needed it, sums up the life of Mary Ann. And it is in this way that she spent her last night of life. Student after student stood up at her memorial service and shared how they had "just spoken with her the night before." In our minds, Mary Ann's life faded away as she walked down the hallway, into the all-consuming darkness. But for a number of students, her life was devoted to them.

And not just to their academics.

Many said that Mary Ann was not only a teacher, but a friend.

This friend, mentor, and teacher set aside the final hours on the eve of her death to build up the next generation of teachers. Of world-changers. Of voices for the voiceless.

At some point, she pulled back her sheets and cozied on up into her bed.

Dreaming, perhaps, about her upcoming move to Colombia. The island. All of the plans and goals and excitement about being around family and golden friends. Of living her love for the Spanish language and her islander people. Of returning her faithful husband to his home, after so many years of his sacrificial living in the United States. Of the people they would need to hire to cut down the bush and transform it into their retirement home. Of the opportunities she already had to speak and teach at Colombian universities, only feigning retirement. Of her hopes to write her stories.

At some point, sleep overcame her and she dreamt her last dreams. Dreams that are a secret between her and her Creator.

Mary Ann rose with the dawn as she did each morning.

She put on her favorite walking clothes, complete with apron, gloves, utility belt, grocery bags, and walking stick. What had once been an opportunity to lose weight had become so much more, her chance to connect with the poorest of poor on the streets of our city. To build relationship with the homeless man in his wheelchair, whom she sometimes helped to get the cans that he couldn't reach at the very bottom of the bin. She had learned the "territories" of these street-dwellers, and made herself one of them from 4am to 6am. Did they have any idea that this white-haired woman donned a PhD? Was a highly esteemed professor at the University up the road? Most likely not. For when Mary Ann was among them, she got just as dirty, just as deep in a garbage dumpster as the next "guy."

People walked by her on the street, during these early morning walks, and yanked their kids away from the "crazy homeless lady" digging through waste receptacles. Little did they know that in about fifteen years, they would be shoving their children in her direction for the cause of higher education.

But this was the kind of education Mary Ann lived for. The real life, day to day, nitty gritty of being what you believed. And she believed that everyone had value. That regardless of your class, color, or status, you were no better than another. There was always something to learn from another. Or so it was with Mary Ann—addict to learning.

And so it was, on her final morning of life—in her final hours of breath—that she went out and mingled with the street-folk. She respected them without patronizing. She loved them without coddling. She rubbed shoulders without regret. She empowered without enabling. She loved like Jesus.

She headed back home...

Walked down the long sidewalk of the cul-de-sac to our house. Smiled as she passed the neighbors' homes, all of who counted her as a friend and confidant. She knew them each by name and would have it no other way. She passed her son's car, a really old Corolla that she and Clinton had sold him to get him started. He had loved it faithfully ever since. She smiled.

Then she passed her new Toyota Prius. The first in many waves of this hybrid vehicle, an opportunity she and Clinton had jumped on for its good value and economic contributions. Just another way to help better the planet. They had saved up and paid for all but the last bit, you know, to keep the credit score impeccable. And, in her stewardly wisdom, purchased life insurance on that car for less than $1 a day. She strolled past the car of her investment in global goodness.

She walked down the side of the house to drop off her bags of cans, bottles, and glass. Added to the mountainous pile of the week's collections thus far. It was Thursday, and in two days, she would take her Prius, fill it with one man's waste but her treasure, and make a good return on it. Perhaps some of the money from this week's collection would go toward helping one of her student's family with groceries—they were really getting low this week, so she had heard.

She pulled off her gloves to open the door.

Stepped inside.

The smell of a cooked egg greeted her. Clinton must be awake.

She turned to close the door, locking it.

And then she was gone.

The sidewalk Mary Ann used to enter the home, moments before dying. She walked in the door on the right, turned and closed it... and was gone.

The room where Mary Ann was killed. The fax machine is in the back, center of the room. Mary Ann died behind the couch on the bottom right of the photo.

Mary Ann was an inspiration to me and knew just how much to challenge me and when to extend her hand to help. I would not be the person I am today without the incredible impact that Mary Ann had on me. Mary Ann was not there as only a teacher, but as a friend who supported me as I pursued my education and who in turn had an impact on all of the students that I have taught for the last four years. Mary Ann will remain alive via all of the teachers that she mentored and in turn the students that these teachers teach.

—*Former student and mentee*

MY HOUSE, A CRIME SCENE

THE POLICE REPORT and court documents agree that Mary Ann most likely did not know what was happening as she was killed.

Her body was lying beside the locked door. The nearby table had been bumped to the side. Blood was splattered onto three walls and the ceiling. One of her eyes was swollen shut.

A bat lay across her body.

A hammer beside her head.

She still wore her walking gear.

Her blood soaked through the carpet into the concrete beneath it.

She was still warm when Jeremy found her there.

He had answered the ringing phone and been told, by the ambulance, to let them in. As he ran from his bed to the front door, the EMTs were already walking in. Clinton had let them in.

Jeremy ran past, sensing that his mom was seriously injured. Down the same hallway that led his mother away from him the night before. "Take care," she had said. He turned the corner, turned another, and there she was. His heart raced, clouding his vision and his thoughts. He knelt beside her.

Still warm.

Turned her face toward him.

A face that would flash into his mind at any given moment, making him lurch as if he had been punched in the stomach. For months, years, this moment would haunt his sleeping and waking hours.

He held her head and knew—she was gone.

Hand covered in blood, wiped on his pajama pants. He grabbed his head and heard a groan come from somewhere deep, deep within him. Maybe even so deep it did not begin physically, a groan from the depths of all things dark and painful and life-threatening. So that the mind closes down to save its host. And so it went, that in a blind fit of grief, Jeremy ran from the house into the front yard, yelling and groaning as only one can do when they have just seen their beaten-to-death mother. Held her face, felt her blood draining from her body.

And guessed that his dad had killed her.

You need to know how much Mary Ann was loved and respected.

For my part, when I saw the article... I felt that a light had gone out of the world, and a very big hole had opened in my heart. But, later I reflected how Mary Ann's presence had been in my life, and in literally hundreds of others, a radiant candle flame. Jesus said that no one lights a lamp and puts it in a place where it is hidden, but instead puts it on its stand, so that those who come in may see it. I was blessed to have been in the presence of her bright light.

Mary Ann used that spark, her inimitable spark, to light the candles of so many others, and although, on this earth, that flame has been extinguished, the candles of all of those who loved, admired, and yes, were a bit awed by her, will burn even more brightly in her honor. She used the talents the Lord gave her and as that servant to whom was entrusted his master's property, took those talents and multiplied them a hundred-fold.

In His presence, she has already heard those words we hope to hear one day, "Well done, good and faithful servant! You have been faithful with a few things; I will put you in charge of many things. Come and share your master's happiness!

—Friend and Colleague of Mary Ann

WHEN YOU GO DOWNTOWN LIKE
THE MOVIES

"Do you know Jesus?" I ask. I cannot get a hold of my pastor so—"

"Yes, I do," she says with a tender smile. "Many of us here follow Him." Relief washes over me. God has sent his angels in police uniform in the midst of this madness.

Jeremy grabs my attention. "Look at my dad's pants," he whispers loudly to me.

It takes a couple slow blinks for the image to sink in. He is splattered with blood from the knee down. No, not just on his pants. His shirt has blood. His hat has blood. His shoes have blood. Head to toe. He is so calm.

Dear God.

The sprinklers come on and we have to move across the street. As we cross, I realize that our entire cul-de-sac is blocked off with caution tape, holding back a barrage of media. Ten to fifteen police cars are parked on our street. Wow. We sit again. I'm still crying.

The phone rings. It's our associate pastor, Josh. The pastor who is expecting us on a flight today. "Josh! I'm so glad you called back. Mary Ann has been... killed. We are sitting on the curb. I have no idea how long this is going to take... What should we do?"

Our pastor and friend listens calmly and patiently. He seems to understand something I do not. And he is gracious. So gracious with my concern about arriving on time for our flight in light of the "situation."

"Marcy, it sounds like you have some things you might need to take care of. I think it's okay if you miss this trip. If you're up for it, I'll meet up with you in ten days and we can go to Paraguay. For now, stay there and take care of Jeremy and your family. We will be praying for you. Do you need anything?" How do I answer that? I need nothing and everything. But mostly, I am just grateful he knows and has freed us from our time constraint.

As if there ever really was one. I think I am the last one to embrace the fact that we are not going to El Salvador today.

The detectives come and say they have to take us "downtown" for questioning. "Downtowns" are real? Wasn't that just on TV? Did we need anything from the house? Dumb questions meant for good. Jeremy gets escorted in to get his shoes.

We walk in slow motion to the far end of the block, passing neighbor after neighbor. The faces and cameras of the media blur into a mob of blacks and grays and whites. Shouldn't it be raining?

We get into a police car. The material of the seat makes me feel like I'm riding on a quarter-type kiddie-ride in the mall. Minus the annoying music and the jerky up and down motions. The wall between the front seat and us leaves little room for knees. I sit sideways. How many criminals have sat in these very seats? Do they think I'm a criminal? What if they never let us out? Bars separate us from our officer who is driving. Jeremy and I are allowed to ride together so long as we do not discuss what has happened. How can we? We don't even know what has happened.

For some reason, the craziest most random thoughts begin to race through a person's head as it tries to grasp the sudden and very immediate transformation their life has just taken. My thoughts fixate on our 11:30 a.m. departure. And—what about the house? I guess I don't need to get our wedding pictures copied for her anymore. Will we be on time for our flight? What about our bags at the house? Good thing we are on the house title, right? Jesus we need you. My thoughts race on in a manic way.

They let us make phone calls as long as we do not say who we think has killed her.

Killed her. She is dead. The words do not make sense.

The phone rings.

"Hello?" Darren answers.

"Darren—Mary Ann is dead—" the words are foreign but bring a sick reality to the moment.

"I cannot hear you, Marcy—what?"

"She is dead—she's been killed—" I choke back my sobs. The words are unbearable.

"Marcy? Did you say something about Mary Ann? You did not say died—you said dead." I hand the phone to Jeremy. I cannot do this. How many times will I have to say it? I cannot say it. She is not dead. She is in her room, getting ready for a day filled with teaching her college kids. Not lying in a puddle of her own blood, possibly flowing because of her husband's hand. Darren was our ride to the airport.

The car seems to drive on a sort of autopilot. I recognize our city's landmarks but they hold no meaning. It's all empty now. We arrive "downtown" and walk like the stunned shocked people we are into a room. The door says "Homicide." Oh God, it is true.

They take us one at a time for our individual investigations. Jeremy goes first. His absence wrenches my heart to its final peaks. What if this is the last time I see him? Will they be able to tell that we didn't do anything? I sob.

I have no clue how long it has been when he returns. I'm immediately traded in his place. Sweet relief. That must mean they know he did not do it.

I am ushered into a dark room with a single light. Wow, I am living inside a Hollywood movie! I'm guided to a small table with the investigator seated on the opposite side. On the table sits an audio recorder. Really? The door closes behind me. A single light keeps the room ominous.

Kind eyes. Sad eyes. A slight smile. I sense a kindness in this man.

Perhaps a sort of chance-friend in this awkward moment. His tone is hushed—almost with a reverence. Or a tenderness that knows that I am on the brink of being swallowed down a very dark and deep hole. And that the future is filled with unimaginable things.

I wish I'd known then how our paths would cross again eight years later.

WHEN YOUR LIFE IS FRONT PAGE NEWS

CLINTON IS ALSO at the station and has been undergoing hours of investigation. It seems like a good sign that Jeremy's wasn't that long. I am asked question after question about this morning, the days leading up, the relationship of my in-laws, anyone I might know with a vendetta against them, against us. I answer as honestly as I know how. I am finally released back to the room with Jeremy.

We sit with Officer Maldonado. An awesome man of faith who encourages us with his story of saving grace. He talks to us as if this whole thing really *is* happening to us. Godly advice on what we do next, thoughts we do not want to think about, funeral homes, telling family, cleaning the house, getting our stuff out of the house, media.

"Media?"

"They will be at your house until 6 or 7 p.m. They know someone has to come home sometime."

Home. Is it home anymore? Can I live there ever again? We call our friend Robert, a man with stature enough to handle the media. Robert happens to answer his phone from the waiting room of the police station. Praise the Lord! We are not alone! "You comin' out or what?" he asks.

"We don't know when we can leave," answers Jeremy.

"Well, the News just said that you two were released without suspicion."

We look at each other. Then at Officer Maldonado. "Can we go now?"

"Yep," he smiles affirmatively. *Thanks for telling us.* Little did we know that the News had been airing our story for quite awhile and was full of more information than even we had. Robert comes back from the waiting room to retrieve us. He leads us confidently through the winding maze of "downtown." Another friend greets us and hands Jeremy a pair of pants.

"How did you know I needed pants?" he asks, still donning his pajama bottoms.

"I saw you on the News—"

We cannot appreciate our freedom any more than we do at this moment.

[Mary Ann] was very special to me. She is one of the two reasons I was able to finish. She became my mentor during some very rough times in my life (bad grades, probationary periods, immaturity, and irresponsibility). She pushed me and supported me so greatly after taking on the challenge. I took her CCC class three times due to failing the first two times... But, God gave me the tools to succeed: I got married, became responsible, and Mary Ann became my advocate/academic advisor.

It was hard to turn the tables around after the damage I did. I earned the highest grades of my college career, graduated, and attended graduate school, thanks to her advocacy. I earned straight A's thereafter. She really impacted me. From the moment I entered and left her classes and office, I was changed, never to view life in the same way.

She had a gift for telling the truth and being provocative. I admired her for being such a brave, kind soul and now, I think to myself...how can I be like that? She was so smart, so involved, so passionate, and I loved her for it...

Thank you for sharing Jesus with me Mary Ann Larsen Pusey. The Christ you shared with me has compelled me to change my life for the better, forever. I'm deeply and truly sorry for your great loss.

—Former Student and Mentee

FIRST DEGREE MURDER

THE FOLLOWING HOURS, days, and weeks were a roller coaster ride.

Clinton was never released without suspicion.

In fact, the doting, gentle, and faithful husband of Mary Ann was charged with her first-degree murder.

His plea? "Not Guilty by Reason of Insanity."

But did he really do it?

This was a question on which the family vacillated. Clinton's family on the island refused to believe their cousin's hand could harm his beloved wife. The Clinton they knew, the intellectual educator, would never do such a thing.

And they were right. He wouldn't.

Not their brother, Clinton. Or their cousin, Clinton.

But this new, more recently strangely paranoid, accusatory, irrational Clinton might have.

If he had not slept in four days due to back pain. And if he had mixed a can of beer with his antidepressants. And if his mind continued to spiral into the grips of Dementia.

Perhaps if these volcanic elements combined to just the right concoction, an explosion might occur. A blackout leaving one's body vacant, except for the very things which have ruled its life for seventy-two years. Like success, power, money—material things attained and guarded.

And this was the case for Clinton. A moral man, Clinton spent all of his years pursuing the belief that "education saves" and focusing on the endeavors of intellect. Believing that more knowledge somehow equated security. Money partnered with power. So that even in his growing insanity, the loosening hold on his own mind led to paranoia surrounding missing money, affairs, and the threat of burglary. Insecurity.

This insecurity consumed his thoughts and ruled his days.

Until he no longer controlled his own thinking and it controlled him.

We considered Clinton's life long and hard. How a man of his moral standing, with a sacrificial love for his wife, and no record of violent behavior in the whole of his past could end up behind bars. A murderer.

His life went against the statistics.

Jeremy began to worry—What if I kill my wife without knowing it? Is that possible? Is it genetic... this thing that has stolen my mom and dad?

Could I kill my wife, too?

One of my favorite photos of Clinton, pre-July 2005.

FRIED EGGS AND ONE MORE THING

CLINTON's only memory of that fateful morning is of cooking an egg, washing his hands, and finding his bludgeoned wife. He remembers calling the police and asking for an ambulance.

And that is it.

He does not remember picking up a bat and hammer.

He cannot explain the splatters of blood on his clothing that occurred within inches of their source.

He is only adamant that he would never kill his wife.

And that he misses her.

For a month, three important things were missing. Mary Ann's wedding ring, another of her favorite rings, and her laptop. The State-assigned defense attorney suggested that someone broke into the house, stole those items, killed Mary Ann with weapons they owned, Clinton standing inches away, then left the house, locking the door behind him.

Or that perhaps the young man who had come the week before to sharpen the Cutco knives for Mary Ann had come back with a vendetta.

"Yeah, maybe he used a Cutco knife," I'd replied.

Or the worst, in order to create a doubt around the Prosecution's offense, maybe Jeremy helped his dad kill his mom.

I'm not kidding.

The defense attorney came into our home and began to ask leading questions. Jeremy was at work and I held this interview alone with the attorney and his assistant.

"Are you insinuating that Jeremy had something to do with his mom's murder?" I asked, beginning to shake. My husband and I were together in bed, woken to a horror, and now he was being thrown in? How does this prove his case that Clinton is innocent?

"It could have been two people," he said. "There are two weapons and your husband had blood on his pajama pants."

I stared at him in disbelief. He knew why there was blood on Jeremy's pants. Every police officer witnessed how it got there... when Jeremy found his mother dead, held her, and wiped his hands off.

"You can leave," I said, firmly escorting the lawyer from my home. I closed the door behind him and wept. Was anyone looking for truth in this case? We needed help, not fantasy.

*T*he laptop and rings were found in a cupboard. The autopsy showed Mary Ann died by being beaten, not stabbed. And the police report showed that a number of officers were in the house and witnessed Jeremy's first glimpse and interaction with his mother.

There was no defense.

*H*is client was proven guilty, we were proven innocent (even though the prosecutor never even questioned our involvement, or charged us of anything).

In fact, in the end, the position of the defense attorney to stretch his imagination and create fictitious situations because his job was to "win" (as opposed to discover and uphold truth) brought me to a sad reality about the state of attorneys.

Or at least that one.

. . .

$\mathcal{T}$hen I considered another Defense Attorney.
And breathed relief to know that His work is based on justice, not "winning," on upholding and fulfilling law, not finding ways around it, and doing what is right for the sake of right, and not the paycheck.

There is one more difference.

This Attorney pleads the cause of his clients, then offers to take their penalty.

Yeah.

He doesn't make it sound less than it is. He doesn't exaggerate what isn't. He doesn't ask for an exception for His clients.

He looks truth in the eye, and when it deserves prison time, he takes it on himself.

If the client will let him.

Imagine this. A murderer stands on trial. The man is guilty and it is proven. The charge is given—along with his punishment. Death.

The attorney looks the judge in the eye. Looks at his client, defeated.

"Your Honor... I'd like to take the punishment on his behalf."

The courtroom is silent.

Then it uproars.

The guilty man just stands there stunned. Could he let this honest attorney take his place? Could he live knowing that this innocent man has died for what he had done? If he returned to his "previous" lifestyle, would any other lawyer ever make this same offer? He imagined only a place like Hell awaited the likes of himself, the gates were within view.

The judge returns the strong gaze of this attorney

"Are you sure about that?" He asks.

The attorney nods. Smiles at the guilty man. Love for another human.

"Then son, you may give your life for his," the Judge answers, tears in His eyes.

The room explodes in confusion. This is not justice! This is—kindness gone too far! Generosity that certainly is not for the pride of the giver. And did the Judge say son? What kind of soap-opera insanity is going on here?

But it is not a soap-opera, though for some, it is insanity.

The bailiff steps forward. Handcuffs the hands of innocence. Opens the door of freedom for the guilty. Ushers the attorney to his fate—his chosen fate. His fate of love for others. Selfless. Unheard of.

This attorney has taught me more than I could ever truly live. Without his constant whispers. His hand in mine. His voice. His tender ways of walking me through life. Never alone.

Not even when he gives his life over for a criminal.

Do you need a Defense Attorney? If you were to stand before a judge, ruling over your thoughts, beliefs, actions, your treatment of others, your taxes, your driving record, every minute of raising your children, marriage, your work life, your honesty, integrity, every exam you ever took, where do you need a defense attorney?

I know a good one.

My dear children, I write this to you so that you will not sin. But if anybody does sin, we have an advocate with the Father—Jesus Christ, the Righteous One. He is the atoning sacrifice for our sins, and not only for ours but also for the sins of the whole world.
—1 John 2:1-2

FIRST TIME BACK HOME. HOME?

THE FIRST TIME we re-entered the house was unforgettable. A moment etched in our minds forever. We entered the mother-in-law suite, suitably named, with our giant of a friend, Robert. One look around told the whole story. The table was pushed from its normal place at an awkward angle, where Mary Ann had fallen into it and crashed to the ground. The walls to our immediate right, straight ahead of us, and even behind us, were splattered with her blood. It was as though someone had brought in a yard sprinkler, set it up in the room attached to the hose, and turned it on. Daring to look up, I saw that even a portion of the ceiling was covered.

I collapsed into Robert, sobbing, "How could someone do this to another human?" Jeremy soaked in the scene, the last image of his mother's face and warm body grabbing hold of his mind. Fitting into its place in this room. His wife being held up by his friend in a room that seemed to threaten to cave in on us.

This was the stuff horror films were made from.

We realized it was time to let everyone know that Mary Ann was gone. To make the phone calls that no one wanted to make. I found Mary Ann's purse. With hands shaking, I dug around the bag to find the address book and planner that Mary Ann kept within. With a sense of violating the privacy of my deceased mother-in-law, I pulled out its contents. An airplane ticket that needed to be refunded. A credit card that demanded a death certificate. Change from her last transaction at the recycling center. A driver's license claiming that Mary Ann still lived and still attained a right to drive her Prius. Her address book.

Not prone to panic attacks, I felt on the verge of what must be considered one. I would never ask Jeremy to make these calls. Robert had recently left the house. I was alone, set to do this task of calling family in Colombia, around the country, around the world. People who loved Mary Ann and Clinton and who would require me to repeat over and over, "Mary Ann is gone…" My mind screamed the insanity of this task at me. Tears ran down my cheeks as I stared hopelessly at the phone book.

"Oh God, please help me."

The doorbell rang.

It was a colleague of Mary Ann's, hoping there was something she could do to help the family of her beloved friend. Indeed there was! Linda also happened to be fluent in Spanish and agreed to make the calls. My tears changed from tears of anguish and despair, to deep gratitude at God's gift and mercy in this moment. An "angel" sent to walk the journey with His children—this broken road at midnight.

We were not alone.

WILL JEREMY KILL ME? JEREMY'S STORY

JEREMY and his father had much in common. They were both gifted in the garden, eloquent in speech and thought, educated and educators, intellectuals.

There was, however, a crucial difference between Jeremy and his father.

Jeremy had accepted Jesus Christ as his Savior. Redeemer. Father. Friend. He said,

---

At the age of eight, in my Sunday School class, I reflected on what my Sunday School teacher had just said. I decided that I did need Jesus and that I would like God to live inside of me. I do not remember really understanding that He had died for my sins and the full extent of what the Gospel message or a full commitment to Jesus meant. I asked Jesus into my heart nonetheless. A year later, after numerous classes, I was baptized in front of the congregation.

My growth in Christ was stunted by the fact that my parents did not take on the responsibility of discipling me. So my discipleship was relegated to Sunday morning flannel board messages that really did not protect me from the influences of the world and an enemy out to destroy my life. My mom was a believer who trusted Jesus Christ as her Savior. As for my father, though, I cannot say the same. He was a moral man of principles and ethics, but he was very much at war with God. He rejected most of the principal tenets of the faith and lived a life based on works. This had a slow but profound influence on me as I developed in my understanding of who God was and His plan for my life.

He had spent many years searching for whatever would fulfill him. He chased after women (and they after him) looking for some solace in the companionship of another human, so long as that human provided comfort and met his needs without much effort needed in return. Each failed relationship, though, convinced him more and more how empty this way of life was. He studied Eastern religions, seeking peace among meditations, quiet living in solitude, and the writings of their founders. He began to use drugs to help him reach an alternate reality where he might commune with the universe and come back whole. Only to find his return to reality endowed with cracks in the mirror of his façade. And it was a façade, an attempt to find what filled him and fully become that thing.

He went to Art school, pursuing his talent in painting, sketching, bronze-casting, throwing his inner world onto a canvas or casted into a mold. Again, the euphoria of drugs helped to elevate him to a level of feigned transcendence—inspiration for his art. He adds:

Through the next five or six years, I was exposed to pornography and a separation between my parents. I reached my first crisis of faith in High School. I decided that I would stop going to church. This produced a habit that eventually led me to reject God altogether during my second year of college. It was then that I slowly started to be exposed to alcohol, marijuana, and tobacco smoking. I got into relationships with women where I lost my virginity and continued in sexual relationships outside of a marriage commitment. My anger and depression that started had now grown to a point where I started to blame Christianity for all of my pain and suffering. In one final lashing out, I rejected God, embracing Eastern religion and cultic practices.

One day, he opened his eyes and saw his life for what it was. Hopeless. Lost. Desperate. He saw the lives of his friends, the deaths of friends too young, the depravity renamed mysticism. He believed there had to be more. He packed his bags and headed to Mexico to find himself.

One afternoon I found myself in Mexico. I was alone in a hotel room. I was seeking meaning to a destroyed life when the Lord directed my thoughts to those childhood seeds... that first love relationship that I'd had with Him as a child. I dropped to my knees in tears and cried out, "God, how I miss knowing you! This is all I ask for, God. I haven't prayed in a long time, but I truly need you right now." I closed my journal and felt a warm presence. I realized there was someone and something supernatural outside of myself. God had reached me in my pit, the pit of self-loathing, but I still did not completely give him my life.

Instead, he found God—in a dream and a vision and terrifying encounters with His counterparts. Unclear on who this revealed god was, Jeremy returned to the US and completed his teaching credential, an ambition to leave behind the ways of his former art-filled life and all of his art with it. He sought this god and found a cult of men instead. Men who declared they had arrived at the truth of all living. That real life, for a man, was to domineer and control women through

115

charm and deception. To prove that you were a real man by attaining the truths of manhood. Success. Power. Control. Meeting around a fire in a deserted location, hooded men huddled to discuss the powers of men and how to employ them.

It took me a year of trying to understand what the truth was about my sinful state and how much I needed to let go. Jesus was faithful though. In the last year before I accepted Jesus as my Lord and Savior, I submitted my mind to a cult where I embraced pagan understandings of living by my own righteousness.

This became his quest. A search for manhood. Something to give himself meaning and purpose amidst millions on a planet, a way to stand out as unique, special, accepted among them all. And it was with a quest of drawing other men into this cult, that Jeremy attended a church.

Well, and to meet women.

He and a friend decided to go to church to meet the ladies and recruit men to their belief system. During their Sunday morning visit, a young man approached them and invited them to a Bible Study. Thinking it another opportunity to scope out women and draw out the men, Jeremy attended. Jeremy said:

But through this cult, God steered me to a Bible Study. It was in this Bible Study that I found men who opened up and were vulnerable... who honestly prayed to God from their hearts. They prayed for each other and cared for each other in a way that only Christ followers can. Soon the Scriptures that they were studying began to open up to me. I began to understand for the first time the Life that comes from the Word of God. The study was in the book of Philippians. Then they reached Philippians 3. Paul says concerning the righteousness, which is the law, that he was considered blameless. But all the things that he found in his previous life were of doing good things and of being righteous were now counted as loss. Rubbish. For the excellence of the knowledge of Christ Jesus, his Lord. This jarred my delusion of self-righteousness... that Jesus was Lord over someone like Paul. It was that night that my whole life flashed before my eyes. I walked around the block for an hour when I came to the realization that Jesus had been trying to reach me for so long. That the God of the universe had been working to save me from myself throughout my whole life.

I continued in this Bible Study, having now finally submitted my life to Christ, and with the help of the Holy Spirit, have been growing in knowledge and discernment of right and wrong. God has sent many mentors and disciplers. Through a slow process of many years, I have grown and continue to be molded as God finishes the good work that He has begun in me.

---

*J*eremy had been pursuing the kind of security this world promises, but so often ends up disappointing and disillusioning. He lived for self and rejected any philosophy that did not support his life mission.

Until one day he saw a man who had achieved it all—and counted it nothing.

Paul.

> *I am not saying this because I am in need, for I have learned*
> *to be content whatever the circumstances. I know what it is*
> *to be in need, and I know what it is to have plenty. I have*
> *learned the secret of being content in any and every*
> *situation, whether well fed or hungry, whether living in*

*plenty or in want. I can do all this through him who gives
me strength.*
—Paul in Philippians 4:11-13

Realizing that no amount of control truly equals a guarantee for joy, happiness, success, or safety, Jeremy handed his life over to the One whose promise stands firm and unshakeable.

As Jeremy contemplated his own ability to kill *me* in a blackout, he embraced the assurance that his life was not his own anyway. That within him, within each person, is the same capability of committing such a travesty against another. We can place our hope in Someone far more capable, trustworthy, and able to bring beauty from ashes than we are. We don't have to fear the things the world fears, because we follow a good God.

Could it be, that the forces that willed you to live one way will control you in such a way later? Does the way your life ends have anything to do with the way one chose to live it? These were questions that we began to ask ourselves, being ever aware that how we live now may affect how we live later.

Jeremy had a lifeline. A way out. An accountability and support that transcended the natural and echoed into eternity.

Come what may, he knew his Creator was guiding and directing his steps.

WHEN DEATH REMINDS US TO LIVE
AND LOVE - MEMORIAL SERVICE

Mary Ann had services in which her loved ones could celebrate and remember her. The first was an informal wake the eve of her actual memorial service.

The wake was held in a large room at the University where she had been working, finishing up her summer courses. On her answering machine at home was phone message after phone message from students the morning of her death, wondering why she was not in class.

Good morning Mary Ann! We are all in class but you are not here. We just wanted to call and see if you slept in, or forgot we have class today... or were just running late. We will wait a bit longer. See you soon.

Mary Ann, we hope everything is okay... it isn't like you to not show up to class without notice. Can you give us a call to let us know you are okay?

Hello Professor Mary Ann... I'm the last one in class now. Everyone else

*left after waiting for about fifteen or twenty minutes. I am worried
about you. Can you call me back and let me know what's going on?*

---

*N*ow they all knew why. The room was filled with students,
university administration, staff, colleagues, family, and
friends. Jeremy and I sat in a bit of a daze while student after student
took to the open mic to share what Mary Ann had done for them, had
meant to them. It was here that we realized just how much more she
had done after walking down the hallway—how her night had only
begun with her "Take care," to us.

Colleagues talked about her passion for social justice, the ways she
stood up against tyranny in the university, vocalized her opinion
about changes that were not beneficial to students or teachers, went
against popular opinion if she believed it was right. Students talked
about how hard her courses were, but how one always left them
changed. They talked about how Mary Ann went above and beyond in
her concern and help for students, offering long hours of phone
conversations, open office hours for mentoring, taking on students as
mentees with topics other professors didn't want to tackle, to deliv-
ering food to students in need.

Mary Ann was unlike any other.

One of her good friends and fellow teachers commented after the
wake, "This was the most inspiring conversation around education
that I have heard in a long time—maybe ever."

On display was a large, framed collage photo display of Mary Ann
throughout her life. In the center was a verse that read:

> *You are the light of the world. A city on a hill cannot be
> hidden. Neither do people light a lamp and put it under a
> bowl. Instead they put it on its stand, and it gives light to
> everyone in the house. In the same way, let your light shine
> before men, that they may see your good deeds and praise
> your Father in heaven" (Matthew 5:14-16).*

Everyone agreed that this verse was suited to the life that Mary Ann had chosen to live, up until her very last breath.

I had undertaken the task of filtering out pictures and sticking them in one of over fifty photo displays on the collage. This had become quite the therapy for me, one filled with many tears, many laughs, and memory after memory as I sat in my own silence and soaked in each image of my mother-in-law, from childhood to her final days. Sometimes I paused to sob and other times the photos seemed to choose themselves and find their place on the display.

Finally complete, I leaned the large frame against the wall. My eyes fell on every single photo: Mary Ann with Clinton, Mary Ann as a child with her siblings and parents, Mary Ann with her kids at their graduations, her own graduations, a life of milestones and accomplishments.

But it wouldn't be the degrees that people would talk about. Or how clean her house was. Few people would mention the many hours she spent on her dissertation or the numerous articles, book chapters, and papers she had written. No, as Mary Ann came up in conversations around the dinner table, while watching the news or reading the paper, or at her memorial services, the discussions would be sure to cover her heart for people, her generosity and kindness, her contagious laughter, and her passion for the underdog. Not that those other things did not matter, but when it came down to what made a person valuable, it is rarely the things we expect. This was also true of Mary Ann. Her worth was not in the stamps of approval the prestigious gave her, but in the grateful souls of those she helped unconditionally.

This was the photo collage on display at the wake and at her Memorial Service. Friends and family passed by it slowly, taking in the many snapshots of a life lived with great intention and purpose. Yes, even her mistakes and failures were signposts on the journey of a life always building and growing into someone who can better serve the hopeless and helpless in the world. Eyes found fresh tears yet again as her smile radiated out from her photos, reminding everyone that life is short and to make the most of what we have.

Clinton's absence from the service was a reminder that our security can never be found in the things of earth. Living a life in search of some security in this lifetime is enough to drive one mad. It also drove home the reality that this gentle man, so deeply committed to his wife, was behind bars for taking her life.

The Memorial Service, the day after the informal wake, found a church packed and bursting at the seams. Emails and cards flooded our home from around the world as family friends heard the news and shared their own grief at hearing such tragedy.

Good friends and colleagues of Mary Ann shared their music, their memories and stories, their sorrow in her celebration. I read two scripture verses that seemed to come up often in conversation when people spoke of Mary Ann and her Savior. Matthew 5:14-16 (above) and Matthew 25:23, "His master replied, 'Well done, good and faithful servant! You have been faithful with a few things; I will put you in charge of many things. Come and share your master's happiness."

Jeremy and his sister shared about Mary Ann's life, as they knew her. One of Mary Ann's sisters shared about growing up with her (and had the room laughing while their tears fell). Colleagues reminisced of passing Mary Ann in the hallway and spontaneous conversations that would come from it, taking massage classes with Mary Ann, or collaborations on ways to change the world, or at the very least, some of the policies at the University.

Finally, to send her loved ones out with joy in the midst of sadness, the attendees sang this song, a favorite of Mary Ann: "You Shall Go Out With Joy / The Trees of The Field."

I've since decided that words of love and affirmation should be spoken when the person is alive, not at their funeral. It's my new mission to say positive thoughts to a person as I think them. Or, as soon as I'm able. Yes, this makes me awkward sometimes. Out of nowhere, I might blurt out how much I appreciate your kindness toward strangers. Your contagious laugh. The way people are drawn to your transparency and it's beautiful. But I'm willing to be awkward to say beautiful truths to the living rather than the dead. I hope Mary Ann knew the many wonderful things people saw in her life.

PAINT COVERED WALLS

I COULD NOT SLEEP.

After staying a couple of weeks in a friend's house, avoiding the media members who stalked our home, we were able to return.

The house now held an eerie silence. Muted, carefully guarding the contents of its secret, the secret of what had actually occurred the night of Mary Ann's death.

If walls could speak...

But they can't. So we re-entered life in this house. Stuck, as it were, because our names were on the title though not on the loan. This ended up being divine providence. Because had our names been on the loan, we would have been immediately responsible for the entirety of the mortgage, which we had presently only been paying half of in rent. Because the loan was not ours, the estate would eventually reimburse us.

However, if our names had not been on the title, the state could have liquidated the home to pay its attorney fees.

Divine intervention, however, is not always convenient or initially seen as the gift it is. We, for the next three years, had to continue to live in and pay for the home of my mother-in-law's murder in order to not lose it.

Each night, as darkness fell on our home and lives, a terror began to fill my heart. I was confident that the one who caused her death was safely behind bars. So why did I feel so terrified?

Jeremy couldn't understand it either. Each night, when I asked him to lock our bedroom door, he would sigh. His grief manifested itself differently—in anger, in sorrow, in regrets.

But for me, much of it came in fear. I realized that while Jeremy and I were sleeping peacefully, assuming the world was a safe and beautiful place, in my most vulnerable and weak state, one of the most violent and dangerous things was occurring yards from my bedroom door. To someone I loved. By someone I loved.

The world was no longer safe. And sleeping even less so.

So every night, for many, many months, I rose obsessively to make sure every single door and window was locked. Including our bedroom door.

Only then, with a silent and desperate prayer on my lips, could I dare to leave control of my awareness for the sake of sleep.

For as it were, this home had many reminders.

Reminders scratched into the ceiling.

Covered by the smell of new paint, new carpet.

Because investigators and police officers only remove bodies, leaving the scene as it is.

And insurance-paid clean up crews only do the bare minimum. In this case, that meant a cheap new carpet for the whole room, to replace the blood soaked one. White paint on blood splattered walls. And scrape marks in the ceiling where the blood-stained stucco had been chipped away. But the drops of blood on the cupboards remained. Little reminders that paint and carpet and a chisel cannot undo the tragedy that they covered.

I sat on the new carpet. The room was now empty of all furniture. The smell of new paint was almost nauseating. Shoot, just sitting in this very room was nauseating. The brain has a brilliant way of trying to fill in the gaps of unknown, replaying over and over all of the possibilities of that morning. I couldn't tear my eyes away from the scrapes in the ceiling. No question, you could still see every splatter, but instead of a red drop, it was a new divot.

I sighed. My breath echoing off the silent walls. The walls that still kept their secret, and now attempted to deny all they'd witnessed with new make up and new aromas. But they were the same walls. Who saw all but spoke nothing. I picked up the can of spray stucco and aimed at all the chiseled gaps. I would join the charade and restore the room to its former self, the pre-death scene self.

When I walked out of the room that morning, it almost looked brand new. The walls were clean, the ceiling scratch-free, and brand new carpet.

Only the cupboards continued to remind the few who dared to look closely that darkness had once had its terrible moment of glory in this place.

TOUCHING DAD

From my journal, July 26, 2005, sitting in an airport on our way to
Paraguay:

CLINTON IS IN JAIL, of course. Last week he fell off of the third tier of a
bunk bed while he was sleeping and woke up in the infirmary. Jeremy
was able to see his dad. He was shaky with a large bump on his head.
His public defender (Clinton has refused every attorney we have sent
to him) called and said he had gone to see Clinton but was told he was
in the infirmary, then the hospital. But, with the Health Insurance
Portability and Accountability Act of California, no one would tell us
anything.

Well, God led us to him. We jumped into the car right away and
had to decide which of the three hospitals to visit first, just hoping
that we would have some way of knowing if he had been admitted.
We decided to start with the hospital closest to us. It was the one!
Clinton was in the Emergency Room. When Jeremy inquired about
his father, the front desk people responded that Clinton had been

admitted. Jeremy explained that he was the son and wanted to know if his father was okay.

The nurse opened the door between the waiting room and the hospital and Clinton was right there in the hallway. Clinton had three police officers around him. Jeremy pinched his sleeping dad (who was just lying on a stretcher in the hallway) to wake him up. Clinton became very agitated that he was in hospital restraints from trying to pull his IVs out. The nurse explained to Jeremy that Clinton had been having seizures and was being monitored. Clinton, still quite agitated at his predicament, declared to the officers, "A man deserves a liberty!" Even in his anger and confusion, he was eloquent. Clinton then turned to Jeremy and told him that he was in the hospital because a guard in the jail had attacked him in the night and punched him in the head. Jeremy leaned over his father, told him he loved him, and kissed him on the forehead.

"I'll see you soon, Dad. They are going to help you. Love you."

Jeremy's prayer from the night before had been answered. "Lord, I want to touch my father at least one more time. Please."

The police officers eventually caught on to what was going on and stated that Clinton was not allowed to have any visitors. We left.

Clinton stayed in the hospital for a couple more days before returning to jail. Of course we weren't given any information.

Except that the blood splatter on Clinton's clothes matched the splatter on the floor. The detective shared with us that if the blood on his clothing had been smeared, it might have been a sign of him trying to help her. The marks on him, however, meant that he had been in the area when the impact occurred. There was no forced entry.

There is no doubt.

We had no idea he could snap like that. He loved her so much. When Jeremy first visited him in jail, Clinton said, "Son, about your mom. I loved her," and began to cry. Jeremy had never seen his father cry until that moment. The next visit was back to his paranoia and delusions. More of his concerns about money and Jeremy's social circle.

I have learned a lot in the last couple of days. We need wills, living trusts, powers of attorney.

And that you have no idea who is going to step up and support your family in your death. It could even be people you do not like.

Life is short and anything can happen.

What will they say about *me*?

Even the prepared and strong die…

10 DAYS IN PARAGUAY

TEN DAYS after Mary Ann died, Jeremy and I were on a plane to Paraguay. Though we had missed the team trip to El Salvador, we were intent on making it to our friends in South America. After a five-hour drive by church bus, we met Pastor Josh in the Los Angeles International Airport. The purpose of this trip had been to introduce the church pastor to the church in Paraguay where I had lived and served during my year engagement to Jeremy. The pastor wanted to see if there was a way to partner with this tiny little church-plant in a Paraguayan barrio.

But now the trip had a second purpose.

To temporarily step out of the daily life of murder, betrayal, confusion, doubt, insecurity, fear, and silence.

The silence that left so much space for questions that could not be answered and regrets that could not be undone.

This trip would allow us some time out of our new element, time to reconnect with friends that were like brothers and sisters in Paraguay, and spend some time processing life away from it.

We were met in Asuncion by the church pastor, Ranulfo. He escorted us back to his barrio by bus. We arrived in his home of wife and ten children, all of whom would sleep in one room so Jeremy, myself, and Pastor Josh could have the other two rooms. I felt life stir up in me again, in a way it hadn't in awhile, and felt a little guilty for it. Was it okay to laugh again with friends? To enter in to life here for this week and forget about the life back home? But life back home would not be forgotten, always clinging to the shadows of our thoughts. Especially when all was quiet.

Jeremy also felt a kind of life stir in him. The piece of him that is deeply Colombian immediately fell in love with these beautiful South Americans and their warm ways. We stayed up late into the night chatting about anything and everything. What takes a typical person three years to accomplish in true friendship with a Paraguayan, Jeremy accomplished in a few days. The Paraguayans welcomed us like their own and I felt a piece of my spirit take a deep, peaceful breath.

How we do life in Paraguay.

In a way, I was home.

These had been my people for a year and I loved them.

Even my dog, Silas.

Who upon seeing me, howled and howled as he embraced me in the way dogs can, on hind legs with head against my chest. He had grown into a full adult-sized dog, though he had once been so small I could carry him in the front pocket of my overalls. He tried to crawl into my lap, which was now half his size, the way he had done day after day a year previously. Regardless of how small his person had become, he made his home entirely in my space. He'd missed me. In my absence, he had taken to being protector and friend to my best human friends, Liz and Oscar and their two children, Tiago and Esteban. This was the least he could do to continue loving his human "mother" while I was away. He did not know why I had left, but he knew I loved him.

He could see in my eyes a new pain, but also love and peace. I was home and he would do his best to ease that sadness.

Silas when he was a puppy.

And that is exactly what Silas did. He did not leave my side except when forced to, but even then, when Jeremy and I emerged from the house in the morning, he was right beside the door waiting. He really liked my new man-person too. Though he had the same kind of sadness in his face, he laughed and played and made himself just like the rest of the people. Yes, he would take this new man-friend of mine and love him equally, because I loved him.

The three of us were inseparable.

Even the following year, when we returned again, Silas did not leave our side. Not when we went to the local school to teach English, not when we went to a family's home for dinner, not when we boarded the bus to a grocery store. This terrified me, as Silas, who was not allowed on the bus, would run alongside it the full length of his doggie territory and then watch it drive off into clouds of dust. He would wait until it made its way back.

Silas coming to school with us to teach English.

I could not wait to introduce Jeremy to Liz and Oscar. They had heard so much about this "prometido" of mine while my teammate and I had lived across the street from them in the little white house. We were the same ages, though Oscar and Liz had a number of years of marriage on Jeremy and me. Liz was my sister in every way but blood. We loved each other like true kin and shared every piece of our lives. I knew that I would tell them what had happened. Why we came with plastered smiles and sadness in their hearts.

Liz and Oscar listened very quietly. Their faces were filled with compassion and shock. They asked questions and took in the story somberly. Yes, even in this most impoverished country in South America, the death of a loved one at the hand of another is a tragedy. Tears were shed and hugs were shared. Oh how I had missed them!

At the end of the week, Jeremy, Pastor Josh, and I gave hugs, cheek kisses, and farewell after farewell with promises of returning in the coming year with a team to begin partnering with the people. Silas was hugged so hard he knew it would be a little while before he would see his person again. His job of protecting my friends would keep him busy until then. He licked my face in his own goodbye and sent me off with a howl.

The Paraguayans had entered into the pain of two North American friends, because distance and time and space and language do not soften the blow of loved ones in distress. Likewise, Jeremy and I entered into the lives of our friends, giving our listening ears and hearts, comfort, and prayers in lavish return to those who had welcomed us with such open arms.

There would always be a piece of this place that spoke home to me, and now to Jeremy. No tragedy could loosen its hold on our hearts.

Silas and I on our first trip after Mary Ann died.

My Paraguayan family - A home away from home.

Silas and I a year after Mary Ann's death.

FLOWERS DIE TOO

THERE IS an empty sort of silence that is left behind when the funeral services are over and everyone is gone.

Everyone.

In the days immediately after Mary Ann's death, the phones were constantly ringing, cards were continually in the mailbox, and flowers were being delivered daily. People even brought meals so that Jeremy, myself, and any visiting family didn't have to think about shopping or cooking amidst all of the planning for services and coping.

Then the services came and ended.

And everything stopped.

The phone was silent.

The mailbox was empty.

The flowers were dead. Just like Mary Ann. There were so many bouquets. They were sent from Sunday school classes, work sites, and friends. They were gorgeous.

But they all eventually died.

And where once stood beauty after beauty now only death was found. Just another reminder that even the most beautiful things die. Flowers had always seemed like a great idea for a gift of sympathy. We were grateful for every one. I determined, however, that I would never send a thing that can die to anyone grieving a death. Why hadn't I thought of that before? Or maybe I would take on the task of throwing out or drying flowers for grievers before the sites of decay joined the scenery of a home in mourning.

And food. There was so much food left over that we invited as many people as would come to share meals with us. Food was so abundant that these invited house guests often left with food in tow as well.

But then they were gone again. And everything was quiet.

A new kind of quiet. The kind that speaks in tones that echo off of walls and leaves a chill in the air. It was the sort of silence that balanced on the beam between inconsolable grief and the rest of the world moving on as normal. Friends could pour their hearts out in a card, put it in the mailbox, and then continue their day as planned. Meet their friends for coffee, buy some groceries on the way home from a day at work, whatever. But we were stuck in a world that wasn't moving and had no sound. At least for a time. Eventually our minds kicked back into gear, life began to move forward, and the silence made way for sounds of everyday living once again.

Our house full of flowers.

WHEN DEATH CALLS US TO LIVE

TRAGEDY HAS a unique way of re-prioritizing life. Things that once seemed important, like putting socks in the hamper rather than beside it on the floor, suddenly take on new meaning. Some things become less important while others grow in significance. This was true for Jeremy and me as well.

Moments that had passed became treasured or regretted. And these memories wove their way into the present, creating a new, intentional way of living in ways that purpose had lacked before. The reality that a "See you later" could become "Goodbye," leads to part-ings with hugs that hold a little tighter, words spoken that may have otherwise remained thoughts, and sincerity that may have once been taken for granted.

Tragedy can also skew priorities.

Two months after Mary Ann passed away, I began my planned Masters program in Rehabilitation Counseling. Mary Ann, a lover of learning, was excited to see me pursuing higher education. The day had come for classes to start, but Mary Ann was not there to cheer me on.

During this program, I had to co-lead a grief group for people who had lost loved ones, namely spouses. I felt it quite ironic that I would aid others in a walk toward healing from their losses when I was in the thick of my own loss. However, by this time, almost a year had passed. And in this year, I had felt an ever-tightening hold on the life of Jeremy.

I had left my job when they began to ask me to participate in interventions that put my own life at risk. Not wanting to bring further grief to Jeremy by dying on the job, I quit. I also began to have frightening fears that he, too, would die, leaving me a young and lonely widow. I was terrorized by nightmares, daymares, and paranoia about an unforeseen, and even unlikely, life without Jeremy. Much of this I kept inside as I put on my game-face and lived life with strength for my grieving husband and family.

I became used to my new role—Supportive Daughter-in-Law. Not a blood child, so my grief went largely unacknowledged. Kind and loving people would approach Jeremy at his mom's memorial, give him hugs and words of condolence, then pass right on by me as I sat at his side. The daughter-in-law. Of one year. How much could I possibly be hurting? Most people in the room knew Mary Ann more deeply than I did, so I would serve as a strong shoulder. And I played my new role well.

On the outside.

On the inside I was terrified that I would lose not only Mary Ann, but her son, and everyone else I loved.

So it was not coincidental, but divine providence, that I walked into the Grief Share group of grieving widows and loved ones to usher them into healing. To walk the journey alongside women living the reality of my greatest fear. It took everything within me to hold myself together during those ninety-minute groups.

But I did.

Only to leave, get in my car, and drive the whole way home, to the house of my mother-in-law's murder, nearly blinded by tears of grief, fear, and pain. Then to pull myself together in order to walk into the house, composed, strong for my husband.

The thing about fear, no matter how rational or irrational it is, is how it debilitates and robs. So not only had my life been robbed of

Mary Ann, but now my life was robbed of many joys, peace, and security as I struggled to function with this new-found fear.

God, in His goodness, never leaves His children to do life on their own, separate from Him, if they do not want to. I didn't want to do life without Him. In fact, if I were able to compose myself and be strong, it was only in the strength that He offered me. My weakness, my fears, my temptations, made much space for His work to shine through. Because it would never be by my own ability that I could offer love to my husband, his family, my clients, if it weren't for the Ever Present Help in times of trouble, who comes to my aid when I was desperate for a way out.

And I was desperate.

Desperate to be okay.

Our church community was a huge piece of our healing.

The Sunday after Mary Ann's death, we quietly attended church, clinging to each other as if one more surprise of any kind could find us in shattered pieces. During the service of one thousand plus people, our Pastor (and friend) paused his message. He briefly informed the church body of the tragedy that had passed before its doors. He asked us to stand.

The entire church stretched out their arms toward us, praying for our hearts to be lifted, for comfort, for peace. Arms stretched in fellowship with the suffering, not hiding faces in fear that tragedy is contagious and to touch us would mean assured losses of their own. No, taking up our burden, our church came alongside and walked through the muck and pain, crying with us, mourning with us, letting what was continue to be. Loss isn't something that can be fixed, and no one tried to fix it. But they prayed.

And their prayers rose to the throne of heaven as a sweet incense, mingling with the tears of a Father found grieving the loss of us, His children. And though our loss was right beside Him, eternally home in His presence, He would trade it for joy and song, He had not forgotten the tragedy that brought her home. The way the broken hearts of His other children grappled to trust Him through this. The travesty of death, death which He conquered and through which He ushered His own into eternal joy, was never meant for people.

His original creation was perfect. Good. But it held a consequence for disobedience. The first man and woman chose that consequence. Chose it. They knew full well that gratifying their selfish desire, prompted by the temptation of another, would lead to death. They had never known death, never seen it among the creatures they cared for. Never tasted it at dinner. And yet, they were told. And they acted nonetheless. Joined the rebellion against the good God who had given them everything they could need or want, including the very breath in their lungs. And the cost of the rebellion was high. Death.

Death entered the perfect world and ravaged the land. Sin entered the hearts of people. This sin, unfettered, led to separation from their Creator. The Creator who wept behind the blazing swords at the loss of His own, as they walked from the protection of His garden, His provision, the ease of the life that they had taken for granted.

Was He not powerful enough to keep them from choosing rebellion? Why allow that thought to ever enter their minds? Why create people at all, only to see them fall and destroy all that was good? These are the big questions that anyone who has suffered at all asks. Sometimes these questions lead people to question the existence of a good God at all, ignorant of His higher ways, His Word, His desperate love.

People only exist because men and women get together and procreate. Mothers and Fathers choose to be parents, knowing that they will encounter rebellion, challenges, and brokenness in the hearts of their children. Why have them then? Yet children continue to be born, even though every person knows that children rebel.

Because children, people, are worth the risk. Some of life's greatest joys and rewards come from raising and loving children. Love. Bringing children into the world gives parents a new expression of their love, for each other, and for the little ones they commit to raise. Children are a gift to the world, even though they will rebel, and are a gift to parents. Yet these "gifts" have a free will, an opportunity to choose to disobey, to walk against the wisdom under which they've been trained, and a right to exist in the midst of it all. Should children cease to exist simply because they will, at some point, rebel? Parents do not think so, for they continue to bear small people within their bodies, bring them into this fallen world, and raise them with great hope, that on the other side of rebellion will be maturity, deep faith, and lives of peace and joy.

So why not allow (as if it is our allowance that is needed) God to create people in the same way? To express His love to the universe, to take the risk of rebellion for the hope of maturity and relationship that may be found on the other side. As opposed to robots who do no wrong yet offer no freely chosen love.

It is through the fallenness of our world that people can see the depth of depravity. The pain of human rebellion against what is right and good reminds us of what we so desperately lack. How large the gap is between our wholeness and what life hands us. Yet the Bible tells us that God is love. And that the greatest act of love is to give one's own life for another. So even in this, our greatest crime against our Creator, God brings beauty from ashes. He offered Himself as payment, laying down His life as Christ, offering to humanity the greatest love that any being can express for another. Our rebellion has been used for good—an opportunity for God's love, the greatest love of all, to be demonstrated and manifested on our behalves in a living and tangible way.

Perhaps it is for this reason that God allowed the first sin to pass before Him, restrained, allowing the painful consequences to fall on His precious ones. Because He saw that in this, He could truly express His love for us. Self-sacrifice. Impossible without someone to die for. So did God bring sin into the world for the sake of love? No. But perhaps He has allowed it, allowed us to suffer, so we can turn our eyes back to Him and find our hope. Find love.

It was this Love that stepped into my fears. Set them aside. Replaced them with peace. Peace that loss, on this earth, is temporary. A blip in the eternal schemes. Because this too will pass. And the pain is real, and the fears will come, but Love is able to conquer and comfort and heal the wounds which fear will keep open and festering.

It was in this spirit, a spirit of desperation for relief and reprieve, that I committed my mind to Love. To seeing its purposes accomplished amidst the trials of life. And setting my heart, not on what is seen—blood splattered walls, headstones, jail bars—but on what is unseen. The behind-the-scenes work of a God who, though allowing such tragedies as these to strike His people, does not leave them to walk it alone.

God did not waste our pain.

He called us to *live*.

A THERAPY NAMED DAISY

ANOTHER DATE NIGHT found us sitting in the large, empty living room. It was furnished but still lacked the life that had once filled it with Mary Ann's laughter, her and Jeremy's playful banter, Clinton's regular television shows.

"Do you want to go to the pound for date night? It might be fun to look at the animals. Ya know, they say that animals are therapy and I could sure use some therapy."

Jeremy looked at me. There was no way we were going to a pound to just "look" at animals. "Marcy, we don't need a pet. If we go, we are going to come home with an animal."

"No we won't," I insisted, "Let's just go look. I haven't been in awhile. Did you have other plans for tonight?" He didn't.

Jeremy hesitantly agreed—so long as we didn't bring one home.

We arrived at the Society For The Prevention Of Cruelty To Animals (SPCA) and walked through the heavy doors. Immediately the strong aroma of dog food and wet dogs greeted us. *Some date night,* thought Jeremy to himself, wandering the halls of abandoned animals. We peeked into cage after cage, me cooing over the cute ones, talking to them as though they understood that this was only a date-night, not a commitment to adopt. We passed through the hall of cats and kittens, most tucked cozily into themselves and their cage-mates.

So far, so good.

After touring about the cages for around an hour, we decided to head out and grab some dinner. As we made our way to the exit, we noticed a small room that we'd missed. Peeking in, we saw just a handful of cages stacked against the wall. Sitting on a table with a worker was the puffiest ball of golden fuzz, tail wagging and eyes excited. "Oh, how cute is that puppy?" I whispered to Jeremy.

The worker glanced at us and smiled. "This is our pet of the week. He just aired on the local news channel and we immediately got a call for his adoption. He'll be going to his new home tomorrow." The golden puppy licked the hand of the worker. She pointed to a cage nearby and said, "That's his sister there. She's not adopted yet."

There was no question why she wasn't picked as "puppy of the week" for the local news spot. She didn't look anything like her brother. His long golden fur stood in contrast to her short, close-to-the skin white fur. As much as he was round, she was scrawny. He was energetic; she was wrapped up tightly, nose tucked into her legs. She glanced up gingerly at us with the slightest wag of the very tip of her tail. She remained huddled in the far back corner of her cage. "This is the sister of that one?" I asked, a bit incredulous. They had nothing in common.

"Yes, they just came in last week," the worker responded.

Jeremy and I continued to peek in at her. She looked lonely. Sad. Did she know her brother was picked and she was not? Did she know her puff ball brother was "puppy of the week," getting opportunities to find a home that she would never have?

"Jeremy, do you think they would let us walk her?" I whispered to him, feeling bad for the sweet puppy with the rotten end of the deal. He sighed softly before asking the worker if we could walk her. Before we knew it, we had the sweet little puppy on the end of a leash. But we were not going anywhere. The puppy wouldn't budge—only cower, looking around in fright. We convinced her with coos, "come here sweetie" and gentle tugs on the leash to walk a couple of feet to a bench. Jeremy and I sat on the bench with our little friend in tow. However, the moment we sat, she skittered under the bench where she continued to cower. My heart felt torn for this sweet little creature—why was she so afraid? Had she seen hard times? Abuse? Abandonment? How did she end up here?

I peered under the bench. "Come here, sweetie. You're okay, come here." I got down on my hands and knees to survey the situation. Big, wide puppy eyes looked back at me, crept slowly toward me. Once she was within reach, I reached in and grabbed her carefully, pulling her out and cradling her in warm arms. The puppy immediately snuggled right in, using my body as her new shield for a painful world. I sat back on the bench beside Jeremy. He reached over and stroked the small dog. She looked up at him, wagged her tail, and licked his hand. I handed the puppy to Jeremy.

Daisy as a puppy.

Jeremy wrapped up the trembling little puppy in his arms. She tucked her nose into the nape of his neck as if he was now the safest place in her little world.

I looked at the two of them. "She is so sweet..." Jeremy laid his cheek on her head. "Can we get her?"

Jeremy had known we would walk away with some animal, but he had no idea how precious, sweet, and life-changing that little creature would be.

We paid for her on the spot and returned for her the next day.

"She looks like a Daisy, huh?" Jeremy asked me. I nodded. Though she was a smooth white, her face lit up our lives like the blossoms of a daisy. She quickly became our "baby" and left her skittish ways behind. Daisy knew she was loved.

And she was brilliant. She was easy to train and could do a handful of tricks. She could shake, sit, stay, lay down—crawl, bark, talk, stand, roll over, and play dead when someone said, "bang!"

But most of all, she just *loved*. Daisy's love language was touch, and she'd take a loving scratch or pat over a bone or treat any day. Except maybe for stuffed animals. A belly rub and a cotton-stuffed anything were Daisy's two pleasures.

That, and laying in the lap of some kind of luxury. Bed, couch, pillows, cushions—she could even manage to snuggle up with a sock if nothing else was around.

Daisy also added a new element of safety to our life. She grew to be medium sized, shaped like a German Shorthaired pointer, freckled like her "mama" Marcy. She was built for running and loved to play chase, yet knew to be gentle with even the tiniest of kiddos. She became nanny to our newborns and toddlers, gracious enough to let them try to ride her, pull on her tail and ears, never flinching or baring teeth.

Daisy was one of the best things that happened to us in those first days after Mary Ann's death. It's true when they say that dogs are a kind of therapy. And Daisy was of the greatest kind. Daisy was sent by God to bring healing to the broken, love to the hurting, companionship for the lonely.

After her time with us (we moved to Germany and couldn't take her), Daisy moved into the home of a family recovering from the miscarriage of their first child. I wept with gratitude at how God's plan is so much bigger than mine. I *knew* Daisy was a gift to us, but I hadn't realized God had another family for her to nurture. Her gift expanded to two families.

Yes, there is life after devastation, and sometimes it comes in the form of a puppy.

MEMORY TREE: A FIRST HOLIDAY

THERE IS LIFE AFTER DEVASTATION, though it takes time before it ever really feels like "normal" life. Even though life will never be "normal" in quite the same way, life begins to take on some semblance of normalcy. Life will never be as it should have been. Sitting around the Christmas tree, handing out presents, will always feel slightly amiss. Like the feeling you have when you walk into a room and have forgotten what brought you there to begin with—and you look around and think: Something isn't right. What am I doing in here? In this same way, celebrating family traditions, looking through photo albums, and the many firsts of marriage found lacking two very special presences: Mary Ann and Clinton.

Jeremy had often called his mom after a bad day in the classroom. Her years in the field of education and her ability to coach students well overflowed into her relationship with her son. She loved that he called her to vent his day, get some feedback, and end the conversation encouraged and ready to try it again the next day. Those phone calls would end with a contented sigh from Jeremy—a new perspective on what had seemed like an eternally frustrating situation.

Then came the first bad day at school after she passed away. The same routine carried on at home—grumbling and processing his day with me. Then came the typical moment when I would have said, "You should call your mom. This sounds like something she could speak into." Those words were silenced, though not absent. They flooded my mind as I grappled for a way to help Jeremy understand his work situation, a workforce foreign to me. *Oh Mary Ann... why aren't you here for a phone call? Your son needs your wisdom and encouragement.* Quiet tears slide down.

Another moment passes where her absence is strongly felt.

Christmas came. Our church held an event called the Memorial Tree. They offered a time for loved ones to come with an ornament to represent someone they've lost. It had been five months since Mary Ann left a crater in our lives. We walked into the beautifully decorated atrium, hand in hand, almost afraid of the pain that might find us here. In such a public place, intentionally remembering the loss can unleash a fragilely controlled dam of hurt, anger, and deep sadness. I was drawn in but hesitant. Why rip a scab off a healing wound?

White Christmas lights streamed along the walls of the dimly lit room, leading us from the door to the brightly lit Christmas tree at the front of the room. A piano sat to its left. Chairs filled the space between us and the tree, with silhouettes of other hurting souls taking time from their lives to remember someone worth remembering. Someone who now, with the passage of time, was acknowledged or mentioned less and less. But never forgotten.

We timidly found empty seats. *Can we possibly belong at an event like this?* I wondered to myself. *Isn't this the kind of event that* other *people go to? The kind of people who lose their mom or dad to some disease of old age, or tragedies that strike other people. Are we really among these broken hearts with our own story?* I looked around at the other faces in the room. The low murmur of conversation adds a sort of anticipatory hum to the room. This place is to remember lost ones—and it's so beautiful. The glowing lights, the festive tree, the decorations of a season full of joy and peace and warmth. And family.

It seems fitting that so much beauty would welcome the hearts of those who come to mourn. Perhaps this is a glimpse of heaven. When the gates are opened wide, and the Son is presented in all His glory.

The light of His face brightens the earth and welcomes the broken hearted, the downcast, the outcast, the forgotten, and the mourner. Heaven is decorated in its entire splendor, ready to receive those for whom the celebration honors. The lost have come home. Jesus stands at the gate, lifting off the yokes of pain, wiping away tears, and trading them in for gladness and joy. He embraces the humbled and broken, lifting them to their feet, and spinning them around in a dance that says, "I have been waiting so long for you! Welcome home, my child. You never have to suffer another day in your life. You made it. Come, eat at my table, and sing with me! Oh, and some people over there want to see you too. They've been waiting."

Out steps smiling person after smiling person. Mother, father, grandparents, friends, co-workers, all with arms wide open and eyes that shine with the light of true life. The friend killed in a car crash looking as radiant and whole as ever. The other friend, killed by a drunk driver, steps over with laughter and hugs. The baby who died in utero—named but never known—perfected, whole, and glorious, calling you by name with hugs of sweet remembrance. The mother, who was like your own, ravaged and stolen by the greed of cancer, stands straight and light on her toes. No pain.

Yes, places of mourning should be dazzling— glimpses of the hope that eternity offers for those who weep. The reminder that one day, every sorrow will be lifted and replaced with unimaginable goodness.

We stood and walked slowly to the front of the room. The hostess smiled warmly, understanding. Her husband had died very suddenly only a couple of years before Mary Ann, leaving her with three young children. Yes, the founder of this event was no stranger to the kind of tragedy and mourning that alters the course of life forever. She handed the microphone over to Jeremy.

He held up our ornament: a silver snowflake with a photo of Clinton and Mary Ann in the last days before her death. "This is our first Christmas without my mother, Mary Ann, and my father, Clinton. She was killed very suddenly in July and my father is incarcerated for her murder. We have come tonight to join with you in remembering the precious time we were given with our family members and friends. Though it ended too quickly, we cherish the time we were given and daily anticipate our reunion. We will spend far more time together than this blip of time apart. I miss my mom, but I will see her again."

The room was quiet. Tears snuck from the corners of eyes throughout the room. Not just because of our story, but for their own stories too. For the lives they shared for too short a time. For the longing in their hearts for one more hug, a chance to say goodbye, the words that were never said. For the hope that the day will come when there is one more hug, no more goodbyes, and everything will be known and understood without words.

One by one, the tree filled up with ornaments.

Hugs were given and received, the tree adornments were admired, and holes in hearts were filled in just a little bit. People walked out the door just a little more full than when they walked in. The longing just a little bit satisfied.

Maybe they got in their last hug after all.

FORGIVING YOUR MOTHER'S
MURDERER - WHO'S ALSO YOUR DAD

JEREMY and I had many visits to the county jail. This was certainly a place that neither of us had ever envisioned visiting. There were two jailhouses in the same vicinity of downtown and Clinton was often moved back and forth between them. Regardless of the exact building, though, the crowd of visitors was always interesting.

We walked in and took a number. People sat all over the room, on benches, on the floor, beneath a television. All with numbers. All with someone behind bars for some crime. Most of the visitors were people that our paths didn't cross on a normal day. The girlfriends of criminals and their children being raised fatherless. Kids running around, playing tag between the trashcan and the pillar in the middle of the room—believing that this was childhood—spent waiting to see daddy when their number was called. Mothers of wayward sons and daughters. Mostly that was it, a lot of women visiting their criminal friends and family.

And then there we were.

I wasn't uncomfortable, except to wonder if people recognized our faces from the news. And often, while waiting, others would ask, "who are you visiting? What are they in for?" When we answered, their eyes looked off distantly for a minute before they responded something like, "Oh yeah—I remember seeing that on the news." We were jail-house celebrities.

At the same time, we found a sort of kinship with these jailhouse waiting room folks. All of them were there to visit someone who had broken the law, and in doing so, been separated from their families and friends. Yet here they all were, trying to maintain a relationship with their loved one.

Just like us.

Which seemed nuts to some. Why would you visit your father after he brutally murdered your mother? It was a valid question.

And we had an answer.

First, Jeremy really wanted to know the spiritual state of his father. He was already 72 and not in great health. "Ah yes," Clinton would say, "My spiritual life. It is good, son, it is good. Jesus is alive. I believe that. Yes, he is alive—just like Ghandi and Mother Teresa. They live on through literature, the stories we share about them. They live on in our memories."

When Jeremy asked his dad about dying, "Are you prepared for death, Dad? Do you know what is going to happen when you die?" The response was always the same. "I have been a good, moral man, son. I have never hurt anyone. When I die, my body will decay and turn into dirt. That is it. But I am not worried, that is how life works."

Every visit, Jeremy shared the Gospel of the living Jesus with his father, not just of the way He lives on in our memories, but of the way He actually *lives*.

"Dad, I just want you to know I forgive you. I forgive you for everything—because I first have experienced the forgiveness of God. I have done a lot of awful things in life. I have hurt people, used people, broken hearts, and God has forgiven me. That humbles me and teaches me how to forgive others as well."

Clinton nodded and smiled and said, "Yes son, of course, yes son."

Secondly, Jeremy really hoped that his father would remember something of that morning and be able to take responsibility for his actions. Jeremy wanted to hear his father say, "I killed your mom and that was wrong. I had no idea what I was doing but I did it, and it has caused so much pain. Will you forgive me?"

But he didn't hear those words. Instead, he heard things through the two-way glass and phone like, "Are you on drugs again Jeremy? You need to stay off the drugs. You also need to come visit me more. A good son would be coming every day and giving me money to buy stamps and envelopes. I have been a good father to you and the least you should do is..." Clinton was belligerent to Jeremy, yet he kept on returning, hoping that this time his dad would remember something and take responsibility.

It seemed hopeless that Clinton would ever have the mental stability to have a truly deep conversation around this topic of faith, forgiveness, life and death. His medication was inadequate while in county jail and because of this, Clinton was not always coherent for very long. But even in his stints of coherency, he clung to his naturalistic views of life and death and did not acknowledge the pain he had caused in his family.

Until one day he did.

Thirteen years later, after settling into new norms within their relationship, a happy peace between them, and properly medicated, Clinton apologized to Jeremy for the pain his actions had caused. Actions he still has no memory of and which still grieve him. An acknowledgment that whatever disorders, diseases, or life decisions had led to that fateful moment, a life was lost, forever taking a mother *and* father from Jeremy. Jeremy had long given up on that moment, embracing that his expectation, his hope, that his dad would remember something of that morning and take responsibility was unrealistic.

But by God's grace.

There's always hope.

WHEN DEATH HEALS FAMILIES

ONE OF THE many things that can bloom from tragedy is closer relationships with family members. Strained relationship brought together with a common sadness, realizing that they have been missing the person they have neglected. Or at the very least, that time is limited and cutting off family for petty things is not worth the loss that comes from never getting to know someone. Crisis is a great opportunity for renewed bonds of friendship.

Or new friends all together.

I had only met Jeremy's extended family after the wedding, in which everything was still a blur and faces blended into memory. Other than that one day, the families had very little contact.

Until the day Mary Ann died.

In the following days, I met aunts, uncles, and numerous cousins from both Clinton and Mary Ann's sides of the family. They drove and flew from around the country to support Jeremy and his sister during the shock of the news, as well as to help get answers as well.

Though horrific circumstances brought them together, friendships blossomed and strained relationships became less strained. Sister hugged sister, cousins hugged cousins, and bygones were bygones. Personalities still sometimes rubbed wrong, disagreements arose, but all of those things were set aside for the common good of the grieving, and with the realization that family is to be enjoyed while one has any. Or time may pass leaving regret in its wake.

The family saw the plight of the newly-made orphans and took us under their wings. Invitations flew in for Christmases in Arizona and Thanksgivings in Oregon. Suddenly, Jeremy and I had more places to be during the holidays than we'd ever had before! We had never fought over where to spend Christmas—our respective parents came together and shared Christmas, making it easy to decide where to go. With Jeremy's parents gone, suddenly there were decisions to be made about where to spend these special days.

Both of our moms and Jeremy during a holiday

The generosity and kindness of our extended family was beautiful. *Why haven't I ever met these people before? They are so lovely*, I thought.

I came from a home where dissension and strife had separated my childhood from any semblance of aunt, uncle, grandma, grandpa or cousin. Very few of my memories include an extended family member. Life consisted entirely of my parents and one sister—that was it. And they were great, but I had often longed for grandparents and cousins. I quietly envied large families who were tight-knit and supportive of another. I knew perfect families didn't exist, but I longed for the opportunity to even have a chance at it.

The death of Mary Ann opened a world of family for me.

And I love them.

But this only came through the tragedy that awakened everyone to the need for intentional friendship within family relations.

Even Jeremy found himself growing in relationship with his own family, some of whom had nearly been strangers previously. Yes, family comes with their hiccups, their growing pains, and their opportunities for growth in how to love others who are different from you. This family was no different, except that they knew first-hand that life can end suddenly, is brutally short, and is worthy of the gems it offers, even if you have to dig through the dirt a bit to get to the treasure.

Even in her death, Mary Ann was bringing people together, seeing to their reconciliation, and cheering them on from afar.

JEREMY AND A ROOM OF VICTIMS

THE TRAGIC LOSS of Mary Ann opened doors of opportunity for Jeremy and me that we never would have had otherwise.

Every year, the Crime Victim Assistance Center hosts a Crimes Victims' Memorial Quilt Unveiling in memory of every person lost to homicide in that year. Each survivor brings in a quilt square that memorializes their lost loved one. They iron on pictures, write verses or quotes, and the dates of their loved one's life. We made a quilt patch for Mary Ann. We ironed on a beautiful photo from her last year of life. She is sitting in a chair, outside, at one of my bridal showers. She has picked up a small container of bubbles and gleefully blows them into the air. I caught this playfulness of my soon-to-be mother-in-law, not realizing to what extent it would sum up the soul of this fine woman. No regard for age, social order or structure, living joy because she knows Jesus, regardless of her share of pain and heartache, this is a moment of celebration. She has met Love. Blowing bubbles.

This moment captured, ironed on, is now a part of the quilt of victims for 2005. It hangs every year at the unveiling of the new quilt of victims. They gather together, each year, to remember loved ones lost to horrific crimes. Rows and rows of quilts, squares of faces and names and lives. She is among them.

Our quilt square to remember Mary Ann.

This particular year, Jeremy was asked by the Victim's Awareness Service to be the keynote speaker. He would be the one to speak to every broken heart in our town—every survivor of a murdered loved one, would sit before Jeremy, hearts open and tender. Their quilt, no respecter of ethnicity, financial status, importance, would hang at his side while he shared his story. Her story. God's story.

Lives woven together in an actual tapestry, people who would never have met, bonded over unexpected grief, a grief that fell on each person in a different way, but tragic nonetheless. Hearts searching for answers, healing, and a place to mourn the injustice that has befallen them. A blanket no one wishes to be plastered on, yet here they were, face after face, celebrating lives taken too early by another's hand. Little in common except for their lives lost, strangers in life but bonded in death. Their families coming together to honor their memories with a small fabric square.

And Jeremy was their speaker.

He began with sharing about the life of his mom, the impact she made on the world and on her community. He talked about the hope that he had because of her faith, his faith, the faith they shared. That they overcome victimization by the power of that common bond, the bond of faith, which transcends any circumstance that happens here.

Jeremy speaking at the Victim's Awareness Quilt Unveiling.

And I have the hope that I will see her again. The end is not with her death, though her loss is felt here in deep ways. My own end will be a new beginning with her, together again, rejoicing that this life has passed and eternity has begun and we are together. Yes, life will have its devastations. Its losses. Its pain. But they are not the sum total of our existence. Our only purpose for living is not suddenly gone, because now we have an experience that brings us to a commonality with many people on our planet. We are not alone in our suffering or our loss. Though the situations in which our loss occurred are wide and deep, the journey from that point on is a shared one. Today we remember and celebrate the irreplaceable lives that we long to see and hug again, to acknowledge the pain of our journey, and to take hold of the Hope that walks with us through such pain until we are reunited with them and our Maker.

The room was silent.

Tears fell quietly from every eye as hearts reached out, desperate to grab hold of the hope that Jeremy talked about. Could there really be life after loss? Can life get better? Should we even dare it? Do we not betray our loved one by laughing again? Is there a place, after death, where we can meet again and forget all of this suffering?

Indeed there is. And it is to this hope that Jeremy and I cling. Not simply for the sake of survival but for the sincere belief that this too shall pass. We thank God, in His kindness, that He will not waste even this pain.

Mary Ann's quilt square is the very bottom right.

HOW ARE YOU OKAY?

WE ALSO FOUND many opportunities among the news media, newspaper journalists and TV station cameramen and newsmen and women, all of whom were biting at the bit to snag this story.

The story of a local university professor, respected among the entire community, slain by her kind, retired intellectual husband without any previous history of domestic violence.

They came to our house, the house of the crime, for pictures, interviews, quotes—whatever they could get that would make a good story. They showed up at the courthouse, camera and lights ready, to be the first to broadcast the next phase of this unique saga.

One particular journalist for the local newspaper, Tim, showed up almost regularly. So often, in fact, that we almost felt like we were old friends. He was very personable and likable, not treating us like the next sound bite or deadline to meet, but actual people going through a tremendous ordeal.

About a week or so after Mary Ann's death, a pregnant Hmong woman and her sister were shot and killed by a drive-by gang member. The women lived in an apartment complex less than a mile from our home. In fact, we passed this complex daily as we drove to accomplish our various errands. A cross, flowers, photos, and a balloon lovingly marked the spot of the demise of these two young ladies and the unborn baby. A young husband survived the pregnant woman. She had been pregnant with their first child. A somber cloud seemed to hang over the small parking lot where the women were killed. Too many deaths in this greater neighborhood in a short time.

Tim had covered the story of these women as well. He had sat in their home, interviewing the surviving husband. The man was completely devastated by his loss and shared as much in his interview. Tim had noted to himself that the man did not look well, and why should he? His entire life had just been slaughtered in front of his meager home. And was there guilt? Was it his gang affiliation that brought about their death? Or was it confusion and miscommunication on the part of the gang that led to the death of the innocent? Whatever the story, the result was the same. A man's entire family was gone in a single instant.

One week after his interview with Tim, that same husband killed himself.

Tim was back with us, sitting on our couch, in the very home where another of his stories had occurred. This was not unusual for him. It was the nature of his job—to scope out crime scenes in hunt for the story. Something to capture and feed to the audience. But something about our family was different. We were definitely sad. Our loss was great. But there was something underlying about us that intrigued him. There was a sort of peace in our home, a comfort and warmth that couldn't be explained, and certainly not in these circumstances. We talked about Mary Ann, about Clinton. We showed him photos and laughed through tears at various memories of Jeremy's mother, her belly laugh, her love for others, her sacrificial living. The mood changed as the topics changed from the details of her death, to recalling stories of her upbringing, to the way she met Clinton and the life of love they had shared together.

There was much we shared with Tim that he wouldn't be able to print. His craft would be to take our words, his other interviews, the evidence—and tell the story the people wanted to read. To answer the questions of the community as best as he could. But there was one question he just had to ask. In sincerity, as if his question was not just for the sake of an article, but of his own curiosity.

"You know, I had an interview with your neighbor over here, the one whose wife was shot in the parking lot. He just killed himself yesterday," he said. "How are you guys... okay? What keeps you from doing the same thing he did?"

For a second, we took in the news of the poor man who took his own life in his grief. "He must not have had any hope left," we concluded.

A friend once said to me, "Marcy, I see that I have suffering, and you have suffering... but your suffering has hope. I want that, too." I wish this man had known hope with his suffering.

Then we began our story. The story of how Christ, in His love for people, offered forgiveness for every crime against heaven. Every act of disobedience, unkindness, selfishness, envy, gluttony, hatred —forgiven.

"If we, who have also wronged others and wronged God, could be extended such forgiveness, such grace as to escape the punishment we are owed, how could we not offer that to Clinton?" we said.

"No, we have not murdered, but in our lifetimes, we have stolen, lied, hated, harbored resentments, lusted after things and people, used others for our own gain, neglected the poor. And for these crimes, we deserve death. Because a perfect God cannot stand in the presence of such wrong. But, this same perfect God, in His love for us, chose not to leave death as our only option. The just Judge wrapped a piece of Himself in flesh, Jesus, sending Him to live among us as a human, because maybe *then* we would listen and believe. But more than that, He knew that only blood could pay for the crimes of humanity. Sheep blood only lasts a little while. His own blood, however, lasts forever. So He gave Himself up, shedding His own human blood as penance for our own fallen natures.

"If the story ended there, there would still be no hope. A dead God who offers forgiveness for our wrongs? But being God, death could not conquer Him. He overcame it in a way none of us ever could. Our punishment had been paid for *and* our God still lives. *This* news is of the 'too good to be true' variety, which is why so many miss it. We feel we *must* pay for our own crimes. Yet here we have someone who has not only offered to take our place, but already done so. All He asks for is our lives in return. It's a win-win! Because giving Him our lives only improves them! So here we are, free from what we deserve, grateful for this mercy that has been handed down to us and now we have a chance to extend that to a fellow human. We pray that Clinton not only comes to understand the power of our forgiveness for him, but even greater, the forgiveness that His loving Father offers eternally—even for this.

"How could we *not* be okay? I mean, this whole thing really sucks and there are lots of tears, and anger, and the 'Why God?' questions, but at the end of the day, while our worlds are rattled, the Word of God is not shaken. It remains true and relevant and provides everything we need to remain whole through a loss like this."

Tim sat back and soaked it in. Of the many interviews he had done after a homicide, he'd never heard anything quite like this. And though only a small blip of this could appear in his article, the rest would settle in his heart and mind and follow him for a long time after.

"HUSBAND'S MIND CLOUDS WIFE'S SLAYING"

By Tim Eberly
May 11, 2006

Clinton Pusey knows his wife was murdered.

And he knows he is accused of killing her.

But he doesn't remember beating Dr. Mary Ann Larsen-Pusey, a retired Fresno Pacific University Professor, to death with a baseball bat and hammer, according to their son.

Now he sits in Fresno County Jail, waiting to be transferred to a psychiatric hospital on the Central California coast, where 73-year-old Clinton will spend the rest of his life if sanity continues to elude him.

Clinton, after pleading not guilty by reason of insanity, has been ruled incompetent to stand trial – a decision that surprised the Fresno Police Department's homicide unit, which described

Clinton as lucid during an interview the day of the murder. His son, Jeremy, says Clinton's mind began deteriorating five years before Mary Ann, 67, was killed in their home.

The changes in Clinton, also a former university professor, began around 2000, after he survived a near-fatal bout with cancer, his family says.

Little by little, paranoia planted bizarre thoughts in his head that Jeremy says he shared with others: The "island people" gave him cancer; people were trying to poison him; the house was bugged.

His behavior became notably worse in July 2004. Clinton and Mary Ann had planned a trip to Clinton's native Colombia. But as the trip neared, Clinton resisted because he believed people were after him.

His family convinced him to go, and things lightened up for a spell.

The following summer, however, Clinton's head again filled with strange thoughts. He removed the license plate from Jeremy's car, saying he did not want people to steal it. He suspected Mary Ann was cheating on him because she had lost 50 pounds.

'Mary Ann is not telling me the whole truth,' he said, according to Jeremy's wife, Marcy. 'She's hiding something from me.'

Not true, says the couple's son, though Mary Ann did keep a secret – Clinton's steady detachment from reality – from the outside world. 'I think she was trying to protect him,' Marcy says.

Jeremy and his wife believe several factors other than his father's mental condition contributed to the attack on his mother. Back pain had kept Clinton from sleeping for a couple of nights. He was also taking several medications, and it had been a week of scorching heat.

Whether those factors played a role or not, Clinton was worse than usual.

'It was very blatant that he needed help,' says Jeremy, 31, an elementary school teacher in Fresno. 'Everything he was saying was kind of fantasy, paranoia.'

The two couples were sharing Clinton and Mary Ann's home on Fresno's Huntington Avenue, as Jeremy and Marcy prepared to buy the home from their parents, who planned to move out of the country.

The night before she died, Mary Ann went into her son's bedroom to say goodnight and bid the young couple well. Their bags already packed, Jeremy and Marcy were flying the next day to El Salvador – and later Paraguay – for a 10-day missionary trip with a church group.

Instead, Clinton woke them up shortly before 7 a.m on July 14, 2005.

'Jeremy, your mom is hurt,' he told them, according to Marcy.

Checking on his mother, Jeremy came upon the grisly crime scene in the garage-turned-apartment where his parents had been staying. Her body was on the floor. He crouched down to revive her, but knew she was dead.

'When I went in there, all I saw was her face,' he says. 'As soon as I touched her body, I knew she was gone.'

He bolted outside, then came back inside and peppered Clinton with questions. He had a gut feeling his father had something to do with it.

'And then I started asking him questions, and he couldn't answer anything,' he says.

Jeremy noticed blood spatter on his father's clothing as police arrived. Officers arrested Clinton and took him to the Police Department for an interview.

Sgt. Dave Madrigal, a supervisor in the homicide unit, described Clinton as 'cooperative and very collected.' He said Clinton appeared to be very clear-headed and mentally competent, but wouldn't say what information he provided.

'The investigators had no idea that he would be incompetent to stand trial,' Madrigal says. 'Nothing stood out. His behavior and actions did not stand out as different from any others who have been arrested for murder.'

A neighbor of the Puseys, Paul Kalinian, also says he never noticed Clinton's mind slipping. Their last conversation was about Clinton and Mary Ann's plan to move that summer to a small island off the coast of Colombia where Clinton was born.

'I have known him for many years. I did not see any kind of abnormality,' Kalinian says. 'If that [his mental state] had changed, I would have noticed it right away.'

Mary Ann's early years were as a poor Nebraska farm girl, Her mother made her dresses from flour sacks.

By the time she became the valedictorian of her high school in the 188-population town of Ruskin, she had read every book in the town's library.

'From early on, she had a thirst for knowledge,' Jeremy says.

Graduating from colleges in Oregon and Kansas did not quench that thirst. She moved to Bogota, Colombia, on a Fulbright scholarship – a government international education program created in the 1940s to promote understanding between the U.S. and other countries. It was one of three she would be awarded.

Mary Ann, fluent in Spanish, fell in love with Colombia and moved back there a few years later.

She held a job at a textbook company. One day, two salesmen strolled in, complaining about a local university professor to whom they were trying to sell books. He had asked questions the salesmen couldn't answer. Mary Ann went to talk to him.

The professor's name was Clinton Pusey.

'I don't know if he bought the textbooks,' Jeremy says of his father, 'but they must have had a good conversation.'

A year of friendship preceded their relationship. They married on June 2, 1973.

Clinton and Mary Ann moved to the United States in 1978 and did something uncommon for that era: They swapped traditional gender roles. She pursued her teaching career while he stayed home to raise their two kids.

'I think she was a person who had so much to give that my dad allowed her to do that,' Jeremy says. 'He took a step sideways so she could become the person she was made to be.'

That person, Jeremy says, was 'a woman of conviction' – a political activist who used her voice to fight against racism and for the underprivileged. A photo that ran in the The Bee in 2001 shows Mary Ann at an organized protest of high energy prices at the Capitol in Sacramento.

She had a Ph.D. in bilingual and multicultural education, but nothing was beneath her, Marcy says. Always a frugal woman, Mary Ann began collecting bottles and cans on early-morning walks several years ago. It brought in some extra money and helped her lose weight. She even had a special outfit to wear while crawling through dumpsters and hauling bags of cans back to the house.

'People would call her names, saying she was a bag lady,' Marcy says, 'But they had no idea this woman had a Ph.D.'

Mary Ann was wearing her recycling clothes when she was killed, Marcy says, leading to the couple's theory that Clinton attacked her when she got home from her morning walk because he mistook her for a burglar.

Since her death, Jeremy and Marcy's faith in God has strengthened, so much so that the sense of loss feels only temporary because they believe they will reunite with Mary Ann some day.

'We live this life and there's something afterwards that's eternal,' Jeremy says, 'I know I'm going to see her again.'

Jeremy's relationship with his father is sometimes awkward. Clinton, though a devoted father, kept his son at an emotional distance. With their 42-year age gap, Jeremy also found it hard to relate to his father.

'Oftentimes, we did not know how to communicate,' he says. 'We did not know how to bridge that middle ground.'

Jeremy has visited his father in jail, and Clinton has called and written letters. He cries a lot, saying he misses Mary Ann.

At times, Jeremy has felt anger toward him, wanting his father to own up to what happened.

'I've had times where I want him to remember,' he says. 'I want him to be able to take responsibility.'

But Clinton says he doesn't have a memory of killing Mary Ann, Jeremy says. Clinton asks: How could I kill my wife?

At Atascadero State Hospital, Jeremy will be able to visit his father without a glass wall between them. But whether that will make a difference in their relationship remains to be seen.

'The dad that I expect is not there,' Jeremy says. 'In a way, I don't know that guy.'

NO MORE DEFENSE

MOST PEOPLE easily grasp the notion that a loss of this nature is devastating. Two loved ones are gone—Mary Ann to life beyond, and Clinton to life behind bars. But unless one has experienced a sudden death, it can be easy to miss the other devastations that follow in its wake. The debt that may be passed down to the next generation. The large number of items to go through, sort, and sell or keep or pass on. The financial burden of memorials, caskets, burials and the fees associated with such. The cost of clean up in the room the crime occurred. Finding, connecting with, and paying for a grief counselor. The sleeplessness, the guilt, the belligerent conversations with a delusional father. All of these and more demand their payment moments after the breath ceases.

In our case, this was no small thing. Still newly married, now responsible for a whole house mortgage on a loan that was not ours, fresh in life and career, we could in no way take on all that death required.

Thus came to life the truth we'd heard over and over—God is an Ever-Present Help in times of trouble (Psalm 46:1).

God's provision of help, ever presently, came through the many donations that poured in from grieving friends and family to help cover costs. It came in through the bureaucracy and laws of California and Victim's Services to cover the $1,000 cost of cremation. Mary Ann's purchase of life insurance on their new car paid it off. Credit cards given a death certificate did not chase us down for final payments. Every financial need was met in its time.

Even decisions about what to do with our home: sell it, hand it over to the government, or keep paying it, were all met with wisdom and direction at the right time. An appointment was set for refinancing the loan, when a friend called with just the right information to alter the course of the meeting.

There was a time during these months and years of consequences that I felt myself the oddball of the family. As different members, my husband included, were tossed back and forth between the thoughts that Clinton killed her or—maybe he did not—I remained steadfast in my thinking.

I had seen the blood on his clothing.

I remembered Jeremy's first words that morning.

The pieces had come together creating a very clear (if not irrational) image of that morning.

Yet two rings (including her wedding ring) and her laptop were still missing.

These were considered valuable and reason enough, according to the defense attorney, for someone to break in, kill a person, and leave, using weapons from within the home and locking the door behind him.

While Clinton stood inches away (according to the investigators who did a splatter analysis).

Leaving Clinton so traumatized that he remembered nothing of the cause of her death.

It was scarcely plausible, but these three missing items were the foundation of the defense attorney's plan to secure Clinton's acquittal.

I felt deeply in my core that these three items were simply missing and had nothing to do with her death or Clinton. So I continued to stay in communication with both the prosecutor and the defense attorney.

It was not to aid the court in condemning Clinton that I carried on in conversation. It was to equip everyone involved with as much information as I could offer to help them find the truth and act on such.

My naivety that lawyers seek truth was frowned upon, but hope against hope I had meetings, phone conversations, and prayer spent seeking the truth and how to help everyone discover what happened that morning.

The defense attorney just could not let the three missing items go. They were his defense.

A weak defense, but all he needed was doubt, not truth, to save his client from a harsher sentence. Or any sentence.

One night during an unusually restful sleep, I dreamed.

Mary Ann and I were sitting at the kitchen table. I was so excited to see Mary Ann again. "Aren't you dead? I thought you were dead! But you are not! You're here! Oh, everyone will be so excited!" Mary Ann smiled her crooked smile. Shook her head. No, she was not here, she was truly gone. But she had a question... what happened?

I realized that Mary Ann had no clue how she had died.

Grateful for this time with her, I regretted having to answer her question.

"Oh Mary Ann... it's a big mess. We can only guess—but you came home from your walk and it is believed that Clinton killed you. He doesn't remember anything, but the scene was awful. I'm so sorry, Mary Ann."

She still smiled, nodding slowly. She did not seem surprised by the information. She seemed only to let the words soak in. She was as beautiful as ever, just as I remembered her. No wounds. Whole.

"Oh, while I have you here... there are three things missing! We can't find your rings or your laptop, do you remember where they are?"

Mary Ann's face lit up. Yes, she did! They were in the house! The dream began to fade in and out as she led me on a tour through the house, leading me to the missing items. She opened a door... was it a real door? The dream flickered. She pointed behind some stored items... "They are there," she was saying, excitedly. "All three are in the house!"

And then she was gone.

My eyes stared blankly at the ceiling of my room. The images of my dream passing before my unseeing gaze.

They were in the house!

God had sent a vision of Mary Ann—a dream—to reveal where the missing items were! I thought of the verses about how God gives people dreams, visions of the night, to warn them. My Ever Present Help in times of trouble. My vision began to clear as the dream faded back into a place of memory rather than reality. But still the message clung to me, pleading—"The items are in the house!"

I sat up slowly, reached over for my journal from the bedside table, and began to record my dream.

When the timing seemed right, and Jeremy seemed receptive, I shared my dream with him as well. He was not opposed to God sending dreams as messages, but he had not personally ever experienced one.

"Let's look again," he said.

So we looked. And looked. And looked. In the same places, over and over, with the same results. No laptop. No rings. I was undeterred. The dream had left me with a solid sense that these items were in the house. I tried to focus on the blurry vision of Mary Ann, her hand on a doorknob... opening a door. Which door? Had we not opened every single door in the house? Shifted through all of their contents? Of which there were many. Mary Ann and Clinton were true to their depression-era selves, hoarding item after item for the "in cases" and "maybes." This definitely slowed the process of searching.

Though we stopped looking physically, my brain continued to wrack itself with memories of the dream and the conviction it had left me with. How I desired to get past these things so the Defense and Prosecution could move on with the real issue. What to do with Clinton and how to help him.

One of Mary Ann's sisters came for a visit to help with going through things in the house as well as attending court proceedings. Though they were often rescheduled for another thirty days out, she faithfully drove the ten-hour drive to support her niece and nephew.

During the next visit of hers, I asked her to keep an eye out for the missing items. Not knowing how this aunt felt about dreams as messages, I shared my sense that the items were here, that Mary Ann had possibly told me through a dream. Our aunt took to her task.

Within minutes she found all three items.

The laptop and the two rings.

The laptop was tucked into the back of a large cupboard in the mother-in-law suite—feet from where Mary Ann's body had lain. It was found behind random other items, in a place where we had looked repeatedly. But today it was there, as it always had been, just beyond our vision and awareness.

The rings were together in a small box of jewelry in Clinton and Mary Ann's room. In the same chest that we had dug through repeatedly. Blinded to the missing treasure, which lay just beneath our fingertips.

Found in minutes.

The mystery was solved.

God is an Ever-Present Help in times of trouble.

I immediately got on the phone and called both attorneys.

"We have found the rings and laptop! They were in the house and we have them! No one stole them, they are here!" My excitement had nothing to do with rings and a laptop, but entirely with the ability for the case to move forward.

To leave behind this false assumption that hindered the progress of truth-seeking in the case of my mother and father-in-law.

"This was the only defense I had," the defense attorney related, exasperated at the find that ruined his plan.

He had nothing left. The evidence spoke for itself. Loudly.

After some deliberation, the defense attorney decided on a new tactic.

Not innocence.

Insanity.

"SPOUSAL MURDER PLEA: NO CONTEST"

Man agrees to first-degree charge; his attorney will argue that he's mentally ill.

By John Ellis
Monday, Sep. 24, 2007

Accused killer Clinton Pusey was scheduled Thursday for a competency hearing in the July 2005 death of his wife, but instead pleaded no contest to a first-degree murder charge.

The new twist means Pusey will move straight to his sentencing hearing, where his attorney will argue that he is mentally ill and deserves to be placed in a state mental hospital such as the one in Atascadero.

"I think this is going to be easy to show," defense attorney Ralph Torres said in an interview. "He's very ill."

Pusey, 74, is accused of beating Mary Ann Larsen-Pusey to death with a baseball bat and hammer. Police officers found Larsen-Pusey, 67, a retired Fresno Pacific University professor, shortly before 7 a.m. July 14, on the floor in the southeast Fresno home where she lived with Clinton Pusey.

Torres said Pusey changed his plea because he admits the crime. But Torres plans to have Pusey's family, as well as Larsen-Pusey's sister, offer testimony on Pusey's behalf at the sentencing hearing.

Prosecutor Robert Romanacce declined to comment other than to say Pusey faces a sentence of 25 years to life when he is sentenced Oct. 12 by Fresno County Superior Court Judge Rosendo Peña. For sentencing, a no contest plea is treated the same as a guilty plea.

Pusey's son has said his father doesn't remember beating Larsen-Pusey to death. He also has said Pusey's mind began deteriorating five years before the crime.

The changes in Pusey, also a former university professor, began after he survived a near-fatal bout with cancer, his family says.

They said he became paranoid and thought people were trying to poison him and that the house was bugged.

On Thursday, Pusey—a native of Colombia—looked frail during a short court appearance. He is in the Fresno County Jail.

He answered questions from Peña in a quiet voice, and there were long periods of silence before he answered a few of the questions.

As part of the no-contest plea, Romanacce said prosecutors would drop two enhancements involving the personal use of a deadly weapon.

"In this case, we have a tragic event," Torres said after the hearing. "The loss of his wife is punishment enough. We need to get [Pusey] to a place where he can live out his life in peace."

INNOCENT BY REASON OF INSANITY

CALIFORNIA HAS A STATE LAW, *Cal Prob Code § 250.* It says:

"A person who feloniously and intentionally kills the decedent is not entitled to any of the following:

(1) Any property, interest, or benefit under a will of the decedent, or a trust created by or for the benefit of the decedent or in which the decedent has an interest, including any general or special power of appointment conferred by the will or trust on the killer and any nomination of the killer as executor, trustee, guardian, or conservator or custodian made by the will or trust.

(2) Any property of the decedent by intestate succession.

(3) Any of the decedent's quasi-community property the killer would otherwise acquire under Section 101 or 102 upon the death of the decedent.

(4) Any property of the decedent under Part 5 (commencing with Section 5700) of Division 5.

(5) Any property of the decedent under Part 3 (commencing with Section 6500) of Division 6.

This became important in the case of Clinton. It became what caused, in part, three years of deliberation.

Could he still benefit from the death of his wife through inheritance? By law, no. The Slayer Statute declares that any person who has killed another cannot inherit from the victim.

But what if they did not know they were killing someone? What if they were totally innocent on the inside? Is that possible?

A family friend (at the time) and civil attorney made it his goal to prove that Clinton could still inherit anything from Mary Ann. In essence, her life insurance, her things would all become his even though his hand took her life.

If he could prove that insanity somehow negated the law.

Meanwhile, the court cases changed from "Did Clinton kill Mary Ann?" to "Did he know what he was doing when he killed her?" Psychiatrist after psychiatrist was court ordered to screen Clinton. Some came back saying that he had early signs of dementia, others stated that he showed no signs of mental instability. During some court cases, Clinton appeared quite put together and coherent. Then there were other sessions.

Sessions where he appeared quite out of sort.

During one such case, Clinton interrupted the judge to ask for justice in a jail-house situation.

"Your Honor, they have bugged my jail cell. They also shoot fumes of some kind into my room while I am trying to sleep. I have had to sleep beneath the television just to stay out of the fumes that they are trying to poison me with. This is not right. A man deserves his dignity. They should not be trying to poison me with their fumes. Not only that, but they come into the room and try to punch me in the head. The guards have no respect for people."

He seemed to be the only one in the courtroom who did not realize how bizarre this information all sounded. The judge responded with a "Thank you, Mr. Pusey, we will look into it." The judge then looked at the defense attorney. "Please silence your client, sir." The defense attorney whispered to Clinton, who continued to carry on about the injustices of his time in jail. Finally the attorney asked him, quietly, to take a seat and allow the Defense to speak on his behalf. Clinton obliged and took a seat. Hands cuffed in front of him. His head and hands had a slight tremble to them.

"He doesn't look good, does he?" I whispered to Jeremy. He shook his head solemnly. At the very least, Clinton had given the media something to work with. Local newsmen and their film crews had set up in various nooks throughout the courtroom. Journalists sat with pens poised, papers shuffling.

Here was the prestigious Mary Ann's husband talking about being bugged, fumes through the vents, sleeping under the television to avoid their conspiracies against him.

Though this time, his room probably was bugged. He was in jail after all.

Was it a ploy to prove insanity? Or true depravity of mind? To this day, the various members in the courtroom would probably offer different opinions. Whatever the case, he pulled it off and the powers that be were convinced enough to allow a plea of Innocent by Reason of Insanity.

The word "innocent" in the plea rubbed me the wrong way.

Innocent by insanity?

Can you truly be innocent of a crime simply because you're nuts? Your brain is so far gone that you commit crimes unaware and that keeps you innocent? I struggled with the legal jargon but kept my lips quiet while my mind soared and fluttered, like an injured bird trying to fly as normal.

The new normal for life was still very uncomfortable. A world where the guilty were proclaimed innocent by their insanity. Slayers could inherit from their slain. Insurance companies cover losses in home due to injury against a homeowner but not by a homeowner.

"FRESNO MAN COULD BE SENTENCED TO MENTAL HOSPITAL FOR KILLING HIS WIFE"

10/12/2007 (KFSN)

A former Fresno teacher convicted of killing his wife has to wait to learn if he'll be sent to a mental hospital.

Friday Clinton Pusey was in a Fresno County courtroom to hear his sentence for the murder of his wife, Doctor Mary Ann Larson-Pusey.

The retired, Fresno Pacific University professor was found beaten to death inside the couple's southeast Fresno home, 2 years ago.

Clinton Pusey pleaded "not guilty by reason of insanity." Both the defense and the prosecution agree Pusey was not aware of his actions when his wife was killed.

Pusey's son says he hopes his father will be sent to a hospital for treatment while the family continues to recover. Jeremy Pusey, defendant's son, says "I maintain constant communication with him and he knows that we're moving on and he's involved with our family still and he knows we pray for him, he knows we love him and he knows we support him."

The Pusey family believes Clinton may suffer from dementia. The judge will wait for a last round of mental evaluations before deciding on a sentence, next month.

"WIFE'S KILLER RULES INSANE: SLAIN FRESNAN'S HUSBAND HEADED FOR A MENTAL INSTITUTION"

By John Ellis
November 15, 2007

A judge Wednesday found that Clinton Pusey, a former university professor, was insane at the time he beat his wife to death with a baseball bat and hammer.

The ruling means Pusey, 74, will almost certainly spend the rest of his life in a mental institution—likely the state hospital in Atascadero—a decision supported not only by prosecutors, but by Pusey's family and relatives of his wife, Mary Ann Larsen-Pusey.

"This is a man who had no rap sheet," said his cousin. "He is not a criminal."

Fresno County Superior Court Judge Rosendo Peña made the decision after a doctor examined Pusey and found he was insane at the time of the July 2005 incident.

Police officers discovered Larsen-Pusey, professor, dead on the floor in the southeast Fresno home where she lived with Clinton Pusey.

Pusey's son has said his father doesn't remember beating

Larsen-Pusey to death. And after Wednesday's hearing, he, along with other family members, all said they loved Clinton Pusey and supported him being sent to a mental hospital instead of being tried for murder.

"In my heart, I know this is what Mary Ann would have wanted," said an emotional family member.

Pusey's family said his mental illness began around 2000 after he survived a near-fatal bout with cancer. As time went on, he became more paranoid. He thought people were trying to poison him and that the house was bugged.

His son, Jeremy Pusey, said Wednesday that the family knew Clinton was mentally ill, but they did not know how to handle it.

"We didn't know it could end up in the circumstances that it did," Jeremy Pusey said.

Pusey had pleaded no contest in September to a first-degree murder charge, and Wednesday was the date scheduled for his sentencing. Despite the plea, defense attorney Ralph Torres had long argued that Pusey was not guilty by reason of insanity, and Peña appointed a doctor to make a recommendation on that matter.

The main concern now, Torres and Pusey's family members said, is to get Pusey out of the Fresno County Jail and to Atascadero as soon as possible.

Peña set a Dec. 12 hearing on the matter but agreed that Pusey did not have to be present. Torres hopes to have Pusey—a native of Colombia—in Atascadero well before that day.

Since his arrest, Pusey has spent more than a year at the state hospital.

"They know him," Torres said of Atascadero officials. "He's been there before. They're expecting him. I expect he would live out the rest of his life there."

Prosecutor Robert Romanacce agreed that Pusey was insane at the time of the murder and now needed to be in a secure facility where he could get treatment and is not a danger to himself or others.

Family members also like Atascadero because they will be able to visit Pusey.

"This is justice," a family member said, echoing thoughts expressed by other family members that Pusey is not a criminal. "We all love Clinton and we all loved Mary Ann. The bottom line has always been we need to do the very best for Clinton."

GOODBYE JAIL, HELLO HOSPITAL

CLINTON WAS CHARGED and sentenced for First Degree Murder with a plea of Not Guilty by Reason of Insanity. He was sentenced to serve 25 years to life for his crime at a State Mental Health facility on the central coast of California. He took one of their 1275 beds, beds reserved for males with mental disabilities posing a threat to themselves or others. The majority of these men are court assigned, as Clinton was.

Regardless of the goal of the civil attorney, the probate courts determined that whether sane or not, a person cannot inherit from a death they inflicted. This meant that Jeremy and his sister would inherit from their mother. The court treated the situation as similar to a divorce, Clinton could keep the half that was his, and the rest would go according to Mary Ann's will, except for any reference to Clinton and inheritance.

Once the courts made this decision, Jeremy and I knew the end was near. Clinton was due to spend the remainder of his days in a hospital that was trained to provide the proper medication for Clinton, something the county jail had been unable to do. Jeremy and I would be able to sell the house and move on—at last. The courts closed the books on the case and we felt some good change on the horizon. Three years had passed since her death.

Three years of jail visits with a belligerent, un-medicated father. A father who had not only murdered his mother, but continued to accuse Jeremy of doing drugs and living a wayward life. A father who demanded more love and support from a broken son, ungrateful for the mercy his family had showed him. Blind to their generous forgiveness of him in spite of his deep grievance.

Then he moved to the state hospital.

They gave him the appropriate medications.

And just like that, he was Clinton again. Humble. Charming. Coherent.

THE COMPLETE CIRCLE: CORBAN'S
BIRTH

THERE IS something about life that sees things come full circle.

When it celebrates and recognizes death's beauty. It is the death of green foliage that once signified the resurrection of spring and the sustenance of summer. The miracles of life now metamorph into brilliant displays of autumn—death's march—not in shades of black and grey but of the brightest, most awe-inspiring shades of victory and praise.

Has the grave ever been celebrated in such a way? With song and proclamation? Yes, a couple of times. Though it is often unrecognized as a celebration of a thing's passing, but of the fruit its death bears.

Without fall, there would be no spring.

Without the expiration of leaves, the rotting of their membranes, the dropping of their seeds—new life could never form. It would be the end, the only end. The final end.

If spring is celebrated, then the death that brought it is also celebrated. To get to the seeds of most fruits and vegetables, one must kill it. The produce is cut from the vine, ending all flow of nutrients and life-giving forces. An incision to the center is carefully carved to get to the heart of the fruit, where often the seeds for new life are stored.

From that one death, comes multiple new lives. Yet seeds alone are not the sole reason for celebration of a fruit or vegetable's death.

The body itself becomes nutrient—life-giving sustenance. Building immunity. Fighting disease. Filling an empty tummy.

A death not wasted.

A death that would have no meaning had the life been spent fruitlessly. Selfishly. Fearfully.

But a gardener spends time with its future harvest: pruning, watering, weeding, de-bugging, feeding with good soil, securing the right kind of sunlight, protecting, caring, clipping. These equate to seasons of dryness, pain, refreshing, rest, growth, and trust. Trust that the gardener knows what to trim away and when.

Trust that the water will come at the perfect time so the roots can dig deeply and with strength.

Trust that the strangling weeds will be noticed. Removed. At just the right time.

I had often watched Jeremy in the garden, cringing when so much beauty was stripped away by his pruning shears, only to see double, triple, quadruple replace his wise and strategic snips.

I watched him allow soil to dry painfully, roots seeking water deeper and deeper, to then lavish the thirsty plant with abundance. Leafy arms raised high, flowery faces turned up, swaying in a dance to their Heavenly Lover—the gardener who knows the whens and the hows and the whys.

And how God has tended to the souls, spirits, minds, bodies of Jeremy and I in the same kind and purposeful way! Allowing us to learn lessons through death and tragedy, lack of understanding, impatience, and frustration, only to be met in those places with every life-giving breath. Sustenance and peace, direction and guidance. Love and affection.

Suddenly life makes sense.

Oh that the garden of one's life would be fruitful to the fullest! So that when every season of spring turns to summer and then to fall, and the hills march to their tune of victory and praise once again, and winter settles upon existence in this place, on this side of eternity, that a new spring would be welcomed in full song! That a great harvest would be found among the seeds of a life—a life not wasted.

God walked us through each season. Held His head high when ours was bowed low. Carried us when we had nothing left to keep us moving. Sang and danced over us when we needed His lullaby. Embraced us with our moments when we could only see unforgiving stone and failures. Then we get to the top.

And He tells us to turn around.

And the view is breathtaking

The most painful of seasons make the most fertile of soil for the growth and harvest in the next.

Even ashes make way for beauty to rise.

To not waste fertile soil of pain in frustration, but to love it for what it will become.

To savor every moment of the blessings given in each season.

To live now—what will living in tomorrow or yesterday give but more regrets and missed moments?

That it's okay to grieve the passing of one season into another, but to offer hospitality to the next season nonetheless.

With joy set before us.

With the hope that every season has its purpose and, when we are willing, each purpose will be accomplished.

So we can live this life fully. Intentionally. Purpose-filled. Joy-filled.

This is the circle of life.

The circle of this season began with the surprise death of our beloved Mary Ann and the arrest of her kind and gentle husband. No one knew the course that line would take nor what beauty would come from those ashes.

But God did.

And we named him Corban Tobias.

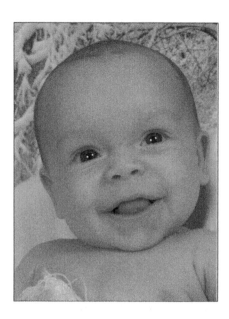

He was born just over three years later in the very home where Mary Ann perished. I labored with my first child for three and a half hours in the very office where our final farewell with Mary Ann had occurred.

The midwife was present. Verses were hung carefully on the wall, reminders that this pain was momentary. A great gift was the result of persevering through the agony of a body dispelling its precious cargo into the arms of his mother. This was a different sort of pain than the pain wrought by tragedy. But the lesson was the same. Endure it, trusting that good is just around the corner.

And he was. Our baby boy was born in water, at home, to the soft sounds of praise music, the dim lighting of dawn streaming in through the window, and a mommy and daddy awake too early for different reasons.

The birth of Mary Ann's first grandchild.

Welcomed in the very place she had been farewelled.

This time the pain, the blood, and the home resulted in a new life, not a lost one.

And then he opened his eyes.

Bright blue lights gazed back into Mommy's greens and Daddy's browns.

There was only one person in either of their families with blue eyes. Mary Ann.

And he remains our only child with blue eyes. A fluke? No. A reminder that once there was death, now there is life. Once there was pain, now there is joy. Our sorrow has been turned into dancing. Our darkness into light.

She is not forgotten and could never be so. But the circle that started with that fateful morning has met an end in new life. In the same place where death took a stand, life now reigns.

We wrapped him in a yellow knitted blanket. A gift.

"Now, no pressure Marcy... but this is a blanket my mom knitted that I'd like to pass on to you for when you have children someday. Really, no pressure. But here it is," and Mary Ann passed the blanket to me. *No pressure, huh?* I laughed to myself. I knew we would have kids someday—or at least hoped so—but not for awhile. I folded the blanket and laid it on a shelf in the closet. Mary Ann died a week later.

And now her precious gift to her first grandchild warmed his little body with more love and affection than yarn alone can do. As if her own arms were reaching down to cradle the young life that now graced her family. How she must have smiled a heavenly smile when little Corban decided he liked recycling cans and bottles in exchange for some money to save up. When he was three and bought his first set of legos with saved up recycling money.

"Corban, your grandma would be proud."

Six year later, walking down the street with our kids, our young son spotted a can in the road. His newest endeavor had been to gather these little gold mines of plastic and tin. He had become keen to the knowledge that one man's litter is another man's cash. He was only three but already understood the value of those little metal coins and the green paper. When you hand them over to people, they give you what you want.

"Mommy! Daddy! Can I go get the can?" We grabbed his hand, stopped and looked both ways, and crossed to get his treasure. He pulled out a plastic bag from his pocket and put the can inside. "I'm going to look for more cans!" Tears pulled at my eyelids.

Oh son, your grandma would be so proud!

And then it hits again. She is gone. She will not be walking her grandson down the street, picking up bottles and cans, explaining the importance of taking care of our earth, getting good exercise, and making some extra change on the side. Even so, this little man-child emanates enough of a grandma he has never met to make it almost feel like she's with them.

Almost.

Mary Ann's grandkids recycling just like she used to!

MARY ANN KEEPS GIVING

THREE YEARS after Mary Ann's death, the courts made their decisions, closed their files, and freed Jeremy and me to move on with our lives. Legally, at least.

Though many new memories were created in the home, Jeremy and I were anxious to leave it behind. Part of the process involved in moving was dispersing Mary Ann and Clinton's belongings to other family members or thrift stores. Lightening the burden that had fallen on us as a young married couple: the burden of stuff.

During our much anticipated house search, I noticed a small photo and brief description of a house in the same area we had been looking. It was way out of our price range but sounded cute, and I was up for looking at it. For fun.

"Do you mind if, on the way to the next house, we pop in and see this one?" I asked our realtor, Ken. He had also been a good friend and colleague of Mary Ann. "I know it is out of our budget, but it sounds nice."

The realtor agreed and drove us into a cul-de-sac of eleven homes. The home of the ad was in the far back right corner, rounding off the block. The front yard was well manicured, filled with rose bushes, berry bushes, and decorative plants.

We stepped inside and fell in love. The first large open window looked into an expansive backyard, filled with greenery and a swimming pool. The living areas were wide open spaces with beautiful sunlight filtering in, quite the contrast from the home of our sorrow, which was not only dark by lack of light but of the memories it contained. We soaked in the warmth of the home while keeping our love for it contained—we couldn't afford it.

The realtor's phone rang. He chatted with a person on the other line while Jeremy and I continued to look around.

"Jeremy, Marcy," called the agent. We walked back to him. "That was the owner, who also happened to be a good friend of your mom's," he said, looking at Jeremy. "In fact, I believe they were co-writing a chapter of a book together. Well, the owners are moving out of state with new jobs. They would like to sell the house quickly. When they found out *you* were just now looking at their house, they dropped the price $50,000."

Jeremy and I blinked.

That brought the house exactly into our house-budget.

"No way," Jeremy said.

"They see it as a gift—a way they can thank your mom for her friendship and all that she did."

We signed a loan and the house papers without any hiccups. Now, without a hitch, the house was ours. We were in awe that God had blessed us with such an amazing gift. We filled all four bedrooms with foster and biological children alike, using our home to bless others in the way that God had blessed us.

We finally had our own home. A home with a legacy of God-fearing owners who had tendered it with care and hospitality, now passed on to us. Who would have thought that the light at the end of our very dark and long tunnel contained a gift like this one? Who knew that another child would be born to us within these very walls? That it would be a refuge to orphans in their distress? A place to splash and play in the pool on a hot summer day with as many families as could squeeze in?

We thought the house was a gift.

It was.

But so were all of the new and beautiful memories that would be created there.

THE GRIEF OF AN ISLAND

THREE YEARS LATER, almost exactly, we decided to visit the island of Clinton's family. We loaded up our almost one-year-old son and nine-year-old foster son (with court permission) and began our journey.

This was the first time that I would meet the islander family of Clinton. Another whole section of family I may never have met if it were not for Mary Ann's death. It was also the first time that Clinton's island family could speak to us face to face about the events of that fateful morning.

Because many of them had known a very different Clinton.

To hear that he had killed his wife was beyond unbelievable to them. They could not understand or accept that their cousin, their brother, their friend could do such a thing to Mary Ann. Their hearts were wrought over the tragedy of their beloved Mary Ann and her Clinton—and had no way of flying to our California home to see it themselves. They had only emails and phone calls to attempt to answer their questions and bring assurance to their mind that indeed, Clinton had done this awful deed.

In the three years that had passed, the information began to settle in their souls and they were ready to begin accepting the facts about the incident.

We stepped from the plane and were immediately received by Jeremy's family. The African features intermingled with the Latin culture was evident on every face, every feature, everything. I looked around and smiled. Everyone looked like Jeremy! Their darkened skin, dark eyes, dark hair, and broad smiles made up the crowds.

Cousins met us at the airport and took us to "Pusey hill" where most of the Pusey family lived. The eight-mile round island knew the name "Pusey" well, better than any other, perhaps. To say, "I am a Pusey" elicits a response like, "I am your cousin!" or "I know your cousin!" Puseys were everywhere.

It was easy to see why Mary Ann had loved the place and why Clinton had longed to return. The Caribbean sea flanked the island with turquoise blues and greens, beckoning sunbathers, fishermen, and snorkelers alike. The reggae beats sounding from storefront shops seemed to sway with the palm trees. Just beyond the shores swam every color of fish, manta rays, and mini sharks. Sunken ships called to every adventurer with fins and a snorkel. It seemed a kind of paradise.

Jeremy sharing his childhood sea with his boys.

Except for the inevitable conversations that would come up.

"How's Clinton?" came the constant question. We did our best to adequately sum up Clinton's state of mind, with tenderness and compassion, easing the load gently onto the hearts and minds of his family. They received it with deep breaths, heavy sighs, and memories of time gone past.

"I just cannot believe this about Clinton. It was definitely not the Clinton we know. Yes, his disease is to blame. Poor Clinton."

We talked long into the night about the events that led up to Mary Ann's death, filling in the black holes of their minds with everything they had not been able to see or know about. His growing paranoia about missing money, accusations of Mary Ann and fictional affairs, even that the islanders wanted to kill him and steal his money. They shook their heads as the stories ebbed and flowed, much like their beloved sea.

We shared conversations over fried fresh fish, grilled to mouth-watering perfection, fried plantains, coconut rice, and fresh cut vegetables. The sun warmed our skin while the stories filled their ears.

They believed.

Against everything they knew about their Clinton, they believed.

They understood the slow decline of his mind, the signs that were clear, but failed to indicate violence, and that everything was being done to help Clinton as could be.

A peace settled on the islanders as they got to know me, the kids, and reconnected with Jeremy. We shared other pieces of our lives as well, the children we brought, our love for culture, and our warm embrace of these far-away islanders who had yet to hear our story from the mouths of Clinton's children.

As if all of this was not sufficient for conversation or picking at the newly scabbed over wounds of our young family, I began to miscarry our second biological child.

ZOE

I HAD ONLY FOUND out five weeks prior to our trip that I was pregnant again. I looked down at my ten-month-old and cried. I was not ready to do this all over again. Yet here I was, looking at a very clear pregnancy test. I knew God must have a plan, so tried very hard to be happy. But deep down, I was angry.

The news began to settle in my heart and I began to accept it. I was pregnant and this would be good—even if it was hard.

At the very onset of our time in Colombia, I began to bleed. The bleeding continued for about one week. But not just bleeding—losing tissue as well. But on the island, in the land of a thick Creole English and Spanish, far from my midwife, I was left to deal with this relatively alone. I feared the worst.

I found a balcony on the third floor of our little rental. Walking through the dusty attic space, I crawled through a small opening that led me to reprieve. The balcony was maybe twice the length of my height. I could see down "Pusey hill" to the ocean as it made its way around this little island. The view was amazing. Only the ocean waves crashing on the shores of the island found their way onto this ledge with me. I leaned against the wall of the house and looked out toward palm trees and sea.

Our little rental house in Colombia where I miscarried Zoe.

Death was on my doorstep yet again—finding me even all the way out on this tiny little island. I needed my Maker.

 rom my journal:

I took the afternoon to be silent before the Lord. But before my time of silence, I begged Him to not punish this child simply because of my own selfishness. Because that is all it truly was. I do not feel ready. I like drinking Pepsi. I like sleeping through the night. I like the small bit of freedom I have just begun to find with my ten-month-old. I was battling this fight over these small things and being quite ungrateful for the gift He was giving me.

So tenderly, He began to show me how ugly my heart had been and He began to clean it up. He spoke gently to my soul and said, "This child has life and is named Zoe because "she" has life. You can't understand what is happening now. I am cleaning house" I heard these words deep in my spirit while the silence I had submitted to blanketed me. They found me in quite the way my Father's voice normally does—in a piece of my soul that is rarely accessed until His voice reveals itself, a voice that crawls through the crannies of my brain and interrupts my thoughts. It comes quietly, but with authority. Tenderly, but with purpose. Thoughts that were not my own, not in my voice or in my usual, selfish way of rationalizing through a situation. For this purpose, for His voice, I silenced myself.

I took those words to mean that through all of the bleeding, this child would live. However, when I got home and visited my doctor, I had a starkly empty womb. The baby had passed away. Knowing that I had heard God speak, I came home and looked up the meaning of Zoe. This is what I found:

"Zoe means life as a principle, life in the absolute sense, life as God has it, that which the Father has in Himself, and which He gave to the Incarnate Son to have in Himself... and of this life men become partakers through faith in the Lord Jesus Christ."(— Vines Complete Expository Dictionary.)

What I realized that day was that God had indeed spoken. Our child is alive... just not in our physical world. Though He removed "her" little body from this planet before her first breath, her life did not end there. It continued on into eternity and she continues to live.

Who knew that such a small child... too small to see with the naked eye, could change my life so profoundly?

One month to the day later, I found out I was pregnant again (all the while trying not to get pregnant!). Obviously God had plans far larger than our human minds could fathom this side of Heaven. Though I did not feel any more ready to be pregnant again, my heart was so restored and redeemed that I anticipated this child with a newfound sense of purpose. God had so intimately prepared the soil of our family that indeed He must have a calling for this young life (and ours).

Our daughter Hannah was born to us one month after Zoe would have been born. In her stead, we are able to love and receive our daughter with gratitude. And as I've heard time and again, we can't imagine life without Hannah. She is a delight to our home, irreplaceable. The news I initially dreaded became one of my greatest joys. How often I have misunderstood God's gift, with a complaining and ungrateful heart, when all the while He had good things planned for me. I've learned to be slow in questioning His gifts.

Zoe's life, physical death, and continued spiritual life were not in vain. Even though there is still so much I don't understand about losing her, God allowed her life to change mine. I can't wait to meet my baby girl in all her glory on the other side.

Until then, her ornament hangs beside Mary Ann on our Christmas tree.

Baby Hannah, born 10 months after Zoe would have been born.

KIDS, MEET YOUR GRANDPA

CLINTON'S new life in the hospital was not amazing, but it was considerably better than his stay in the county jail.

In the hospital, Clinton had his own room, hot meals, a chance to walk outdoors in the prison garden, see the sky and get fresh air. None of this had been possible in the jail. He was also able to be adequately medicated, which seemed to ease his tremors, return some of his lost weight, and give him clarity of thought. We could send him packages and often did. We sent him photos, books and any other things he might ask for.

On one occasion, Clinton asked for a Bible.

With large print.

I quickly got online and had one mailed directly to him.

Many months and many visits passed.

Then came the first visit with our children.

Because of the Swine Flu pandemic, the hospital had closed down visits to anyone under the age of eighteen. Clinton had read in letters that a first grandson had been born to him, but could not meet him with the restriction on children in place.

As soon as it was lifted, Clinton met his grandson.

Jeremy and I went through the very thorough process of signing in, waiting, passing through security, putting coins in baggies, and waiting in the meeting area. A small, square-shaped room provided a place for families to meet with their imprisoned loved ones. No two-way windows or bars between them. The security guards saw that the rules were followed—a hug was okay on the way in and out, but no excessive touching. Clinton was not be allowed to hold his grandchildren, but he could hug them and see them, give high-fives, and talk. This was more than Jeremy or I had ever thought possible. But here we were.

Jeremy and I worked hard to keep our toddler and foster son (now son) occupied while we waited. Clinton walked into the room. His eyes fell on the two young faces sitting at the table with us.

"Dad, I would like to introduce you to your grandson, Corban. And this is our foster son, Matthew."

A photo of our first visit with Clinton in the state hospital.

Clinton's face lit up as he hugged his grandson for the first time. I sat beside him and snuck Corban onto his lap. Perhaps his only opportunity to hold his grandson. Clinton beamed. He found his "daddy" voice and cooed and coddled our little one. He looked up at our foster child and asked him about school, friends, his grades, took an interest in this young boy too. Eventually the guard noticed Clinton holding Corban and reminded us that he could not hold any of the children. I took Corban back, grateful for the time I had been able to give my father-in-law.

Then it struck me.

Grateful? That the murderer of my mother-in-law could hold my son? Would Corban ever understand how his mother willingly handed him over to the man who killed his grandmother? Ah, but he is so much more than a murderer.

He is forgiven.

Just as we are.

Forgiveness didn't make the event disappear or Mary Ann return to life. It did not mean that Jeremy and I wished for opportunities for Clinton to unintentionally hurt others again. It simply meant he was more than a killer. More than all of his failures. And he could still be loved. This was one way of loving him, to allow him to hold and see his grandchildren.

We paid for a Polaroid picture and captured the moment in that prison-hospital's visitor room.

We continued to visit so that our children could know their grandfather.

Then Liz joined our family. Then Hannah.

Now with four, Jeremy and I walked into the waiting room, ready to introduce him to two more grandchildren. Liz and Matt's adoptions had just finalized. Hannah was now born.

Clinton walked into the waiting room, as usual. He looked up at his waiting family, saw two new beautiful members, and began to weep. He sat down at the table with us, head in his hands, and sobbed. Who was he to be so blessed?

During one meeting, Jeremy again asked about his dad's spiritual health. Clinton responded, "It is good! I have been attending the church in the hospital here, and reading the Bible you have sent me.

God is so good to me. Often throughout the day, a song will come up out of me, a praise song for God. The words are not always the same, but the tune is always similar."

And with that, he began to sing. His deep voice unabashedly sang out the truths of his soul in his mother tongue, Spanish. This time, he sang not of a Jesus who only lives on in our memories, but of a Savior, a Redeemer, a Forgiver... who stands at the right hand of God and gives us every good gift.

He had met the Savior.

Clinton meeting his two newest grandchildren.

Another visit with grandpa!

On a visit with Clinton during a summer trip home from Germany.

AND THEN THERE'S HOPE: A NOTE
FROM JEREMY

I GET ASKED OFTEN how or if I have dealt with my mother's death.

On the morning of July 14th, 2005, four days before my first wedding anniversary, I was startled out of my sleep by a bloodied father who had just bludgeoned my mother to death on the other side of our house. That morning I came up against the biggest and toughest trial I had faced in my life to that point. This tragedy became public news and took three entire years for any official closure with the courts of justice. The effects of that day have rippled their way through my and my family's lives.

How can someone go through something so horrific and still function properly? How? Yes, the effects of this tragedy still ripple through my life daily, but my response and my resolve may come as a surprise or a confirmation depending on your own personal faith perspective.

My response from the beginning was defined by my faith in God. A God who, in a very real and vivid way, revealed to me that He exists and that He is a rewarder of those who earnestly seek Him. This revelation came through the divine yet human person of Jesus Christ. Years before the tragedy, I had put my life and trust in the hands of this man, born around 2000 years ago, who lived a perfect life. He was killed and miraculously came back to life. His life and His legacy changed history, the world, and most importantly, my life.

I had faced other trials and painful experiences leading up to the one shared here. I had seen firsthand how my trust in His wisdom and in His truth could bring me through an array of experiences. As a Christian, my example, my model, is Jesus.

His life and example show me how to die without blaming anyone, even the ones who caused his death. Was it not He who asked God to forgive those people? Was it not He who said they did not know what they were doing?

If my mom's murder cannot be understood, then at least it can be brought into the light of this truth. Death is a part of this life. It is a part of the depravity that is found in every human, including myself, and in this case, manifested in the actions of my dad. My mom's life was destined to end. Our lives are destined to end as well.

The tragedy is not in the means by which she died, but in the greatest curse of human existence, death. But the hope lies in a future that Christ ushered in. The Bible speaks of this promise, "Death is swallowed up in victory" (1 Cor. 15:54). Both Satan, who had the power of death (Heb. 2:14), and death itself, will have been cast into the lake of fire (20:10, 14).

My mom shared this belief in Jesus Christ. In a variety of ways throughout our relationship she affirmed a trust in His promises. Jesus Christ's promises, in a very real and extraordinary way, an eternal life for those who trust in Him by renouncing their lives and following Him.

That very real promise is what helps me understand that our relationship did not end with her sudden departure. Because of this hope, my mom's departure from this life was like leaving a room. Someday I will follow her into that next room and be reunited with her forever more. What crazy hope you might say! I call it the Hope that Jesus brought to the world; hope that so many reject because they cannot believe in a God who would be that generous. As for me, my trust is in the LORD.

I hope that you do not mistake my words for some shallow Christian-ese lingo that paints a rosy picture of a very wounding reality. This Hope guides me! Heaven! Psychiatrists pine and travel far and wide through the human psyche trying to help people find this hope.

I went through grief counseling. For six months my wife and I met with her in a tiny office where we dealt with the tough process of grief. I want to credit her for making me face emotions that I did not want to deal with. She mirrored back the pain and loss that everyone naturally goes through when faced with a tragedy like the one I was facing. In our sessions, I came to understand the very real human emotions of the grief cycle. I went through anger at the situation; anger at the loss. Sometimes I had anger with my parents and their lives leading up to the event. Sometimes turning my anger into blaming them for the pain I was feeling.

Sometimes my grief veered into denial. I did not want to face the fact that my mom was dead. Or if not face it, feel it. Many witnessed, including my wife, a deep sadness (depression, my counselor would say) I faced for a time. But through this journey of mourning there was always a light through the pitfalls and dark alleys of emotion. A light the Bible declares so vividly. There will come a time when I will not have to deal with sadness, with disappointment, with pain. There will be no tears of misfortune, tears over lost love, tears of remorse, tears of regret, tears over the death of loved ones, or tears for any other reason. There will come a time when I will see those who went before me. There will come a time when I will understand fully what happened and why it happened.

I believe in a God that is perfect, loving, and in full control of my life. There is nothing that happens without his consent or that surprises Him. I believe in this God that promises that He will never leave me nor forsake me. That "our light and momentary troubles are achieving for us an eternal glory that far outweighs them all" (2 Corinthians 4:17).

"...We know that the one who raised the Lord Jesus from the dead will also raise us with Jesus and present us with you in his presence. All this is for your benefit, so that the grace that is reaching more and more people may cause thanksgiving to overflow to the glory of God.

Therefore we do not lose heart. Though outwardly we are wasting away, yet inwardly we are being renewed day by day. For our light and momentary troubles are achieving for us an eternal glory that far outweighs them all. So we fix our eyes not on what is seen, but on what is unseen. For what is seen is temporary, but what is unseen is eternal. (2 Corinthians 4:14-18)

It is hard to sum up in words all the ways God has carried me through my mom's murder and my dad's incarceration. I can only do my best to present to you that it is Christ in my life that keeps me going. It is His life, His hope, His understanding that sustains me. My mourning is a lifelong journey and will not be resolved with a quick fix method or a life of denial. Though I hope you see that my faith gives me the tremendous ability to endure suffering and pain. To contextualize life as a journey that treats pain and suffering as what it is: real and inevitable.

And then there is Hope...

Jeremy with his mom at a graduation ceremony where she taught.

AFTERWORD

LIFE AFTER DEATH

THE WISDOM OF LIVING ASSUMPTION-FREE, trust-filled, and believing in more than I can see. This, I believe, is one of the greatest lessons I have learned. One that has spared me many undue heartaches. One that I wish I'd learned much sooner... but am grateful to have learned at all.

To take in a circumstance with all that my eyes, ears, and heart can understand, and then believe that there is more to it than I can know, and to rest in the assurance that Someone knows. It doesn't have to be me.

Though I often wish it were.

How easy it is to look at a weed—one sole weed—and determine that the entire garden must be over-ridden with this decrepit beauty-choker. What frustration, hopelessness, and despair could overwhelm me if I never looked up.

Never looked up to see a beautifully flourishing garden, weed-free.

To pull just one weed and be at ease.

One weed at a time.

Or maybe it is not a weed.

But a miscarriage. Financial loss. Death of a loved one. Disease. A broken relationship. An unexpected bill.

A friend's comment. Or lack of comment.

An envied gift given to another.

Whatever it may be, it's an opportunity to allow that one moment to suck you in and convince you that God is dead, life is unworthy of living, and what you see is all there is, and it is unexplainable. Unacceptable. Unlivable.

Oh how I have bore up under these moments! These lies! When I was convinced that death was far better than life! That God must hate me. That no one loves me. Not one.

Only to have my head lifted.

To see a garden—beautiful, weed-free—goodness that overwhelms a moment. A circumstance. A broken expectation.

To see that her death changed more lives than her life had, because of her life lived, then given over.

To realize the unspoken comment was not absent from mind and heart, just air.

That the loss of what I thought I wanted and needed was not what I wanted or needed, and I was free from the tangle.

To hand over something I did want knowing that I can be better without it.

To surrender what I see and trade it in for the hope of what is unseen. The knowledge that is unknown.

To recognize the command as an invitation, the discipline as life-sparing.

To see what once seemed like hate, not as hate, but of a very hard love. A love needed to see true change. The hardest kind of love, but the truest.

To live a life that trusts the unseen, that believes and hopes in the greater, that refuses to waste pain for the greatness that can come from it. To be mastered by no moment, no fickle feeling, no thing that we have established as greater than we are.

Save One.

The One who sees all, knows all, understands all, offers all.

For free.

To rest in the assurance that I am loved and all is for my good. What a life of peace and security!

God has taught me this, through difficult lessons, unexpected surprises, moment of humility and regret at having jumped to conclusions.

May this be a lesson I continue to grasp, in every moment of every day, and live out in such a way that the world around me releases the hold of false assumptions, accusation, self-absorbed thinking, generalizations of each moment onto every moment.

And meet my God.

Because He'd love to show you His garden.

Your garden.

> *Trust in the Lord with all your heart and lean not on your*
> *own understanding; in all your ways acknowledge him,*
> *and he will make your paths straight. Do not be wise in*
> *your own eyes; fear the Lord and shun evil. This will bring*
> *health to your body and nourishment to your bones.*
> —*Proverbs 3:5-8*

ANGELS UNAWARE

YEARS LATER, sitting at my computer in Germany, a message comes up.

A member from our home church says that the detective from Clinton's case is trying to reach us.

Memories flood back.

It's been eight years, and still the feelings can rush back at the slightest shift in weather, smell, or sound, triggering a million memories.

Curious, I copy and paste the email address and reach out to the investigator.

The one whose dim bulb lit our conversation in the downtown police station.

"This is Jeremy and Marcy Pusey—we got word from our home church that you were looking to contact us regarding an upcoming hearing of Clinton Pusey. We are living out of the country at the moment. You can respond to us here..."

In less than an hour I have a reply.

"I don't know if you remember me but I was the lead detective on Clinton's case. I retired from the police department and now work for the District Attorney's office. I am also a member of your home church and knew you and your family were in Germany… I'm being told there is a possibility he might be released from custody."

What the heck?

"Yes, I was the one who spoke to both of you at your home and at police headquarters. When I first saw you at church, I didn't know if it was okay to talk to you due to my role in the case."

Two things happen in this moment.

First, I am overwhelmed and in awe of the ways God cares for us. Little did I know, when I was in the darkest part of my soul's despair, weeping in a room with a stranger, fear-filled and confused, that God has sent me one of His own. The man who held my number, who was assigned the role of finding the truth in our case, was an image-bearer of Truth Himself, gifted with His Spirit to discern rightly. And not only a man of God, but a man from our church! From our own community.

I sit back and let the reality wash over me.

When I felt alone and afraid and out of control, God was with me, brave, and sovereign. And in His kindness, He sent us a detective from among our own flock. And we had no idea.

The whole time, every Sunday, that we were watched, cared for, prayed for by the detective on our case.

It's a moment when I realize just how deeply and radically loved I am.

The next thing that happens a small flurry of panic. Clinton might be released from custody? A strange dance stirs up in my spirit. A dance of peace and joy at God's goodness and a writhing fear from deep within that this world is still too unpredictable, unsafe, and I somehow have to fix it.

Peace wins.

His faithfulness overwhelms my fear. If He was good eight years ago in a darkened room where my fate and my husband's fate hung on the line, isn't He faithful now? Is He big enough to deal with a court's decision for my father-in-law? Is He for me or against me? Is He for or against Clinton? Had He not just sent us the same detective to walk us through a new possibility? A comfort settles my soul.

It's okay. We're okay. God will never leave us nor forsake us.

Little did I know how beautiful and precious the court's decision would be for our family.

EXPANDING HEART AND HOME:
ADOPTION

JEREMY and I had always had hearts for children. Even before marriage, we had talked about our desire to one day foster, and possibly adopt children. In some ways, we felt it our duty to offer a good home to others in need of one, especially kids.

We also felt compelled by love to do so.

Remembering our own adoption into God's family drove us to replicate His love to others in need. So we went through the process of certification to foster through a local faith-based agency. We gave no specific parameters, willing to take anyone who needed our love.

Then came our first foster child. He was eight years old and needed a home for the weekend.

A year and a half later, he was adopted as our son.

Then came five other foster children—a teen mother, two little boys, a teenage girl—all needing love, all accepting it in different ways. Or not accepting it at all. Because being available to help an orphan in distress does not always "save" the orphan. Sometimes their trauma and their free-will collide and lead them away from everything good and down the same dark paths others before them took.

Then came a student in Jeremy's class. She was eight years old. He had been her teacher for two years, in second and third grade. During a parent-teacher conference, her foster mother shared that she had too many kids in the home. This particular child would be moving to a new home when the county could find one for her.

"I would take her," was Jeremy's impulsive response. And he would. He did.

This sweet girl joined our family of three (by this time) and became our forever daughter.

A way to follow in the footsteps of our Maker, and his mother. A way to be a voice to the voiceless, help to the helpless, comfort to the downtrodden, and security for the out-of-control.

In a year and a half, our little family grew from two to six. Corban was three-months-old when Matthew, our first foster child, joined us. Then came and went five others for various seasons and chapters. Liz joined our home, followed by the birth of Hannah one month later.

Mary Ann would be proud.

The day we became the legal mom and dad of our two oldest children.

From my journal:

These things always cause me to pause and reflect on three adoptions, those of my two oldest children, and my own.

Jeremy and I adopted two children out of the foster care system. We'd had each of them for a number of years before the adoptions finalized the role we had already claimed in their lives: mother and father.

We stood before a judge.

We swore an oath—to love them, to give them full rights as legal heirs, to be their mommy and daddy.

They swore an oath of agreement, my then eleven-year-old and nine-year-old.

They were given new names.

A new birth certificate.

My name. Jeremy's name. Their names. As though it had happened this way at birth.

Had always been this way.

I remember the tears in the judge's eyes, as she stamped her approval. Her seal. Making it all official.

The other four days of her work week look a lot different— dealing with parents who have lost their children, are not fulfilling the "simple" tasks being requested of them, seeing families fall apart.

One day a week she brings them together.

Adoption.

It was final! No more having to ask permission to leave the city! No more needing court permission to get certain medical needs met! No more being forced to do things that we felt were against their best interest, just because the system had deemed it so for everyone. No more wondering if we would give up on them too, send them on their way, kick them out of our family. Our commitment to be their forever parents.

A blessing and a challenge.

These two kids have radically changed my life. They've brought about the maturity I lacked as a person. They have brought me to my knees, desperate for the guidance of Jesus, on so many occasions. They have made me laugh, cry—put to test everything I have learned as a counselor.

They have been gracious with me, merciful even, as I have learned to parent older children. My imperfections—so evident— are handled with love and care.

And then I stop.

And remember the day.

That I stood before God. My Dad. The Judge.

And swore an oath.

To be His child forever. To let Him be my Daddy always.

And my name was changed.

My certificate renewed.

Sealed.

Tears in eyes.

Security. Knowing I would never be alone again. Left out again. Outcasted again.

I have a forever-home.

And oh! How I must make him laugh, cry, and, if He has any grey hairs, how I must have contributed to them! He has been so patient, consistent, loving, gracious, merciful, tender—

And never ever gone back on His oath.

Removed the seal.

Called me by my former name.

Not.

Once.

Even when I have failed miserably. He smiles, picks me up. Helps me with the next step.

Oh that I could be that same kind of parent! To smile, pick up, and help. Instead of criticize, judge, and modify. To set aside myself and simply be about them. And who they are. And who they are going to be. And not how it makes me feel or inconveniences my moment.

Even now that I am a parent, my Dad still continues to be my greatest lesson, my greatest example of how to love all, regardless of blood or "good behavior" or what is deserved or not.

To open my arms wide to all who need a forever home, a forever heart, a forever love.

To be a shelter for the lost, food for the hungry, a comfort to the downtrodden and beaten.

To aid the orphans in their distress.

As He has come to the aid of this orphan in distress.

My forever-home.

For all who are led by the Spirit of God are children of God. So you have not received a spirit that makes you fearful slaves. Instead, you received God's Spirit when he adopted you as his own children. Now we call him, "Abba, Father."For his Spirit joins with our spirit to affirm that we are God's children.
—Romans 8:14-16

"FORMER PROFESSOR ACCUSED IN WIFE'S DEATH RETURNS TO FRESNO"

By Marc Benjamin
February 03, 2015

Clinton Pusey, who beat his wife to death in 2005 and was found not guilty of the crime by reason of insanity, has been released to a halfway house in Fresno County.

Pusey, 82 and a former student adviser at Fresno Pacific University, was released Monday. When his insanity was determined in November 2007, it was expected that Pusey would live out his days in Atascadero State Hospital. But under state law, Pusey was eligible for release once his sanity was determined to be restored.

During court hearings, Pusey didn't recall beating his wife, Mary Ann Larsen-Pusey, 67, to death with a baseball bat and a hammer, said his lawyer, Ralph Torres. She was a former Fresno Pacific professor.

Torres said Pusey's family knew he loved his wife and came to his defense in court hearings. Prosecutors, Pusey's family and his wife's family all supported Fresno County Superior Court Judge Rosendo Peña's finding of insanity.

Pusey's family said his mental health had been deteriorating for five years after he survived a near-fatal bout with cancer. They said he grew increasingly paranoid and thought people were trying to poison him and that his house was bugged.

When he was sent to Atascadero in 2007, he was "a fragile old man," Torres said.

Torres said Pusey and his wife had plans to return to Pusey's native Colombia in their retirement.

"He was sick when I had him," Torres said. "They gave him medicine that made him sane, so he deserves to get out."

A BEACH HOUSE AND 12 YEARS

IT'S 12 years to the day.

Some of it feels as fresh as yesterday... the memories of that morning: Mary Ann a blur on the ground, Clinton's disconnection from his surroundings, his hat to his shoes covered in the splatter of blood, the hard seats of the police car, and the endless weeping.

There are still days when it hits me and I cry anew. When I look at my kids and feel the loss of a woman they never got to know. When Jeremy wants to process his life as an educator or remember certain beliefs she held. Would they have changed and developed over 13 years? I've learned that the philosophies you hold the day you die become yours forever. Even re-reading this book, which has been ten years in the making, takes me right back to some of the hardest moments of pain and moments of deep, awe-filled joy.

And other days it feels so distant. Like a movie I once watched about someone else's life. It's become normal in ways a story like ours should never become normal. But life carries on. We've experienced new traumas since this first one, so fresh into marriage and young adulthood. We've raised children of trauma and live with the realities of Reactive Attachment Disorder and dysfunctional attachment. We've survived near-divorce and post traumatic stress. We've experienced deeply toxic and wounding work environments and relationships. We've lost too-young friends to cancer and death.

Sometimes it feels like the break of waves hitting the shore, one despair after another. But it also feels like the eye of a storm where life swirls and whirls and threatens around you, but you're safe in the center of something you have no control of. This I can only ascribe to God. A peace like no other in the world. A peace that has held us so tightly in the midst of hurricanes, earthquakes, floods. He has given me more than I can bear but has never left me alone to bear it.

We've had many moments of against-all-odds miracles and moving mountains. Moments that exceeded any dream or expectation or hope.

One of these happened in July of 2017.

We, our four children, their aunt, and Clinton stayed for a week together in a beach house... over the 12th anniversary of Mary Ann's death.

The timing was not planned.

We never saw a day in our future where we'd spend any time with Clinton outside of an institution. But a few years ago, the courts deemed Clinton harmless enough to be released to a Con-Rep program. He lives in a supervised home in a regular city, with freedoms to come and go, so long as he is consistent with his medication, his group therapy, his individual therapy, and any other expectations.

He's 85 years old now and definitely slowing down. I was not comfortable with Clinton being released to this program, but now I'm grateful. It has given us opportunities we thought had died with Mary Ann.

The week together was incredible. It was a divine dance of hard and good. Healing and re-wounding. Fearful and peaceful. I won't lie and say it didn't cross my mind to worry that my sweet mother-in-law's murderer was sleeping down the hall from my vulnerable children. I won't deny that I prayed for God's peace to sleep well and shields of impenetrable protection around my children and family.

My children got to spend time with their grandpa. Not "the man who killed my grandma" but just Grandpa Clinton. They got to know his humor, his precious accent, his laugh.

One night over dinner, he paused to say affirming statements to each of us. What he saw in us that delighted him. How beautiful or handsome we are. How smart and creative. I sat in stunned silence. Even as I type, my eyes well with tears. That a man who was broken and condemned would share our table and home and speak blessings over us.

Just Jesus.

I imagine this is a picture hard for some people to understand. "Why in the *world* would you want to sit around the table with a man who brutally killed someone? Why would you let your kids sleep next door? Why would you ever talk to him again?"

Jeremy summed this up well in his final note, "And Then There's Hope." Some things can't be explained. God's peace is one of them. As we've chosen to follow His peace into uncomfortable places, we've experienced redemption, healing, and reconciliation, the kind that needs to be in the news more often. The kind we can't fabricate or orchestrate. It's beyond us. We were front-page news for three years because of a murder, and not at all for the redemption.

But this journey is also my own sin reflected. My own reconciliation reflected. I haven't killed anyone, no... but as a high schooler, I fantasized about killing the bullies who wouldn't let me go. I drew comics of their death, a twisted way of bringing an end to my pain. A false end. I as good as murdered them in my heart. I've lied. Stolen. Manipulated. Used my words to wound. Schemed for my way to be done. Been arrogant and proud. Lusted after the affections of men. How many mistakes until I'm irredeemable?

Even one separates me from a perfect God.

But not even a million would keep Him from redeeming my willing heart.

.   .   .

*C*an anything ever separate us from Christ's love? Does it mean he no longer loves us if we have trouble or calamity, or are persecuted, or hungry, or destitute, or in danger, or threatened with death? (As the Scriptures say,

> For your sake we are killed every day; we are being
> slaughtered like sheep. No, despite all these things,
> overwhelming victory is ours through Christ, who loved us.
> And I am convinced that nothing can ever separate us
> from God's love. Neither death nor life, neither angels nor
> demons, neither our fears for today nor our worries about
> tomorrow—not even the powers of hell can separate us
> from God's love. No power in the sky above or in the earth
> below—indeed, nothing in all creation will ever be able to
> separate us from the love of God that is revealed in Christ
> Jesus our Lord.
> —Romans 8:35-39

*C*linton once told me he'd only live to 85 years old.
He's now 86.

I don't know the time he has left, but it's caused me to be mindful to mark the moments we have. To give our lives permission to interweave and carry on a story of Glory that only one author can write.

"And then," in the famous words of my wise husband, "there's hope."

*Just returned from our week together, our first time together outside of jail or the state
hospital in 12 years.*

LETTER TO MARY ANN'S
GRANDCHILDREN

Dear Matthew, Elisabetta, Corban, and Hannah,

Your grandmother, Mary Ann Larsen-Pusey, was a dear friend of mine. Whenever I look at your family photo on my refrigerator I am reminded of her and of how proud I know she would be of each one of you, her grandchildren. I'm sorry that you will not get to know her and that she never knew you. So here are a few things about her so that you can know what she was like.

Mary Ann was, most of all, a passionate and loving woman who spoke her mind and who spoke from her heart even when others disagreed with her. In faculty meetings at Fresno Pacific University where she taught, she would burst out with her ideas. When she agreed with someone, she would let them know; when she disagreed with them, she would say so. However, more than anyone I have known, she never let her strong beliefs keep her from loving others, even when they disagreed with her or were angry with her for being candid and honest with her opinions on an issue. That is the single biggest thing that I learned from Mary

Ann. Whenever I'm upset with someone and wish I didn't have to talk to them, I often think of Mary Ann and how she responded with love toward everyone.

Mary Ann believed strongly that there should be justice for everyone and committed herself to working for peace and justice in her community. She never wavered when defending anyone who was being mistreated or overlooked. One example of that is this:

In the city of Fresno, there is an invisible line. North of that line live most of the city's wealthiest people and south of it reside the poorest people. Throughout the 1990s and 2000s Fresno's businesses continually closed their doors and moved north where the money was. This left the poorer neighborhoods with very few stores and services. Mary Ann steadfastly refused to shop "north of Shaw." She stood in solidarity with the poorest members of the Fresno community. She believed that Jesus would have cared about the poorer neighborhoods; to my knowledge she never broke this vow. It was a matter of her faith and conscience.

I loved Mary Ann's gruff voice and gravelly laugh. I loved how her laughter burst from her with delight at the world around her. She loved everyone and listened to what they had to say. She even delighted in the environment and streets of southeast Fresno. She was always picking up trash or encouraging people to recycle.

If Mary Ann were alive, I know that she would be a steadfast supporter of each of you – the strongest supporter you could want. I'm not sure that she would have been the kind of grandmother who would play with you or make cookies for you. However, I am certain that she would have listened carefully to what you have to say, she would have been interested in all your ideas and activities, and she would have laughed heartily at your jokes. Most of all, she would have encouraged you to find your own path in life, helped you to understand what you are feeling and thinking, and supported you at times when you need to make difficult decisions or when you have to stand up for what you believe. She would have let you know that she understands you when you are unsure of yourself or have doubts about your faith. She would have listened to your fears and loved you.

If Mary Ann had been granted the opportunity to live and to meet you, she would have been the grandmother sitting in the audience or the stands of every play or sport or event that you ever participated in. And she would be cheering you on with all her energetic and raucous laughter and encouragement–and you would have loved it, but also you would have rolled your eyes in slight exasperation, laughing with each other about how embarrassing Grandma could be. That is my image of her now, loving her grandchildren as boisterously as possible and encouraging them along the way.

It is my hope and prayer that you can feel her love for you and her pride in you even though you will never meet her. The spirit and joy of your grandmother lives on in your dad and your mom, in your aunt, and in every one of us who knew her.

I'd love to meet you all sometime. I'd like to know what things you care about and how you view the world around you. Who knows; perhaps we'll meet sometime.

I wish each one of you a life of peace, contentment and deep faith – the kind your grandmother experienced and would wish for you.

Sincerely,
Hope

IN MARY ANN'S WORDS

In Mary Ann's own words, written in 1996 for a presentation at the University.

Following Norm Rempel is not an easy thing to do. I am not nearly as funny as he is; though I am from Nebraska. He said he is a BIG RED fan, I am not. In fact, I don't care much for football at all. However, right after we bought a car from my sister in 1993, Norm tracked me down by the bumper sticker she had on it. It reads; I have two favorite teams. Nebraska and whoever plays Oklahoma. I am not sure if he even wanted to know I was from Nebraska or that I had spent the worst year of my life in Oklahoma! By the way, my husband drives that car, not me!!

Planning for this profile has been almost as tough as when I applied for a position here in 1990. At that time, I was told to plan a 30-minute talk summarizing my spiritual, educational, family and professional pilgrimage. This time I was told I had 35 minutes. Summing up my life is hard to do. You'd understand if you saw my "hoja de vida." In professional circles we call it a curriculum vitae—a way of listing all of the things you have done in your educational and professional life. Mine is nearly 12 pages long; it takes two pages just to list all the places I have studied and worked. Anyone looking at it would decide that I like change or at least I should be comfortable with change.

I have been told that most people don't like to get out of their comfort zone or that change causes stress. I have a hard time understanding that. I thrive on change! Change keeps me on the cutting edge!! It keeps me from getting bored or stagnant. I never want to be accused of being like the Dead Sea. Finding change in the same place is hard, so I have moved around a lot—I have lived, studied and/or worked in seven of the 50 states and four states in Colombia. I have also traveled in six other countries, in every state west of the Mississippi River, and in every state of Colombia except two.

In all these changes, God has taught me a great deal throughout my life and I want to share with you some of the things I have learned through the people I have found in these many places. Living among strangers has meant changes in how I define community now and how I used to define it. It also means that my perceptions of people have been altered. First impressions can be important and used to be very important; now I realize I can't judge people so easily and that first impressions can be wrong. Living in lots of different places not only has meant changes in the way I view people but also what I understand community to be.

I am not sure why I like change so much. Maybe it has something to do with being the oldest daughter of an immigrant. My dad left Denmark at the age of 30 coming to Nebraska. He had planned on entering seminary but found he needed to know English to do that so he ended up as a farmer, the occupation he had left behind in Denmark because he didn't like it. Or maybe I like change because my maternal grandfather had three brothers who had what my mother always called the wanderlust—they left home as young men and only one of them ever came back.

Uncle Wilhelm died under strange circumstances and my grandfather had to travel to Missouri to identify his body which he was able to do by the Schiermeyer hammer toe. I heard that story for the first time when my son inherited that hammer toe. Another became somewhat infamous. At family reunions there is always a wall with newspaper clippings and old letters telling of the adventures of my mother's Uncle August. He once edited a small-town newspaper. He was a member of the IWW and he was even elected King of the Hoboes.

Uncle Fred left school after three days insisting he knew more than the teacher did. When I was four, he stayed with us for six months. I can still remember how exciting his stories about riding the rails to different places all over the United States to find work and adventure were. Or maybe I like change because we moved four times before I was nine years old—who knows!! Maybe God just made me a pilgrim on a journey through this world, a person who wants to experience as much as I can.

I once challenged a student who thought she had moved a lot in her life to match my record. When I counted up the number of different mailing addresses I have had in my life, I found there were 42. And that doesn't include hotels where I spent less than a month in traveling. The longest period of my time I have ever lived in one place was nine years: from third grade through high school graduation. Four or five years is about my tenure in a place and then I get itchy fit. I either have to move or find some other ways to incorporate change into my life. We've been in the Valley now for seven years—four in Merced and three in Fresno. My husband and kids have insisted that I put down roots so I guess I will stay awhile. I will have to find a new way of finding change.

I have lived in the country, in small towns, medium-sized cities, and huge metropolises like Cali and Bogota, Colombia, and San Diego, California. I was born and raised on the farm. Before my 10th birthday we had lived on three different farms in northeast Nebraska. I started to school in a one-room country school. We moved to a farm near Ruskin, Nebraska, in March of my third grade. Ruskin was and is an unincorporated village of around 150 people. I only experienced multiple-grade classrooms including in high school. I had 10th grade English before my 9th grade English and Algebra before Geometry. There were 45 in the high school the year I graduated in a class of eight. My brother and I went through school together and managed to keep the academic honors in the family. He was salutatorian and I was the valedictorian!! I don't know that he has ever forgiven me for having 4/10 of a percentage more than he did in my GPA.

I don't know that growing up I thought much about the concept of community. I don't think that community was important to my father. He never met a stranger in his life. On the other hand, my mom needed friends and support but she thought that community was found in family. That was why we moved from northeast Nebraska to Ruskin, so that we could live near her family.

In reviewing my life with the concept of community as a theme, I have come to realize that one can find community among those who are most like us and will fail to find community among those who are very different from us. Over the years, I have not found that to be necessarily true. Sometimes, I have found community in the place I least expected to find it and didn't find it were I thought for sure I would find it.

I can't say that the community that I grew up in was a typical one. In some ways, it was a close-knit community but it could certainly exclude some people. Until I left this country, I assumed that every small rural community in this country was like it. If someone had a disaster, people dropped their own work to rally around the person who needed help—yet it was also a community which was very closed-minded.

Until I lived in Portland, Oregon, I thought the only kind of prejudice that existed was religious. I remember a man from the community who married a Mexican-American woman who had a son from a previous marriage. The community was horrified, not because she was Hispanic, but because she was Catholic. As soon as she was converted to the Lutheran church, the community accepted her. Yet, they refused to accept the three or four families who went to the non-denominational church in town. You had to be Lutheran and yet even then there were exclusions.

I remember the big fight at my high school baccalaureate service. The three ministers in town took turns, but we wanted the father of one of the boys in our class who was the pastor of the Danish Lutheran church to give the invocation and it wasn't his turn. We asked the minister of the German Lutheran church whose turn it was to give the benediction. He refused to take part because he said he couldn't pray with someone who wasn't from the same synod that he was!

When I was twelve I had polio and spent three months in a hospital. One would think that community would be hard to find in such a place, but it wasn't.

I grew up in a Christian home and upon high school graduation left Nebraska with no intentions of ever returning. I entered Multnomah School of the Bible in Portland, Oregon. Among very conservative Christians with whom I shared faith and much more, I expected to be accepted as I hadn't been in my very Lutheran community. But I wasn't. To this day, I am not sure why. Was it a cultural difference? I was only one of two mid-westerners. Most of the students were from Washington, Oregon or California.

So after I received my diploma in 1959, I went back to the state I had sworn to never set foot in again! For three years I worked for Back to the Bible Broadcast in Lincoln, Nebraska. Again among strangers but ones with whom I shared faith, I was sure I would find community. I did, but not where I thought I would. I found my niche in a small Mennonite Brethren church near one of the four different mailing addresses I had during my three years in Lincoln. I had met up with Mennonites at church camp as a child, through Mennonite Disaster Service, and in Bible School in Oregon. I found them to be interesting people; they were the first church group I had found who really lived what they talked. Here were people who would take off from work without pay to go help rebuild a town destroyed by a tornado. That was new to me.

In the churches where I had been involved up to that time, I had heard a lot of "preaching" but had not seen a lot of "living." For three years I enjoyed a sense of community with an exciting group of young people in that church. And because of those contacts, I ended up going to Tabor College to finish up a degree. Being a secretary and proofreader was getting boring!!

At Tabor College I was again among strangers, though strangers with whom I should have had a lot in common. But try as I might I couldn't find community where I expected to find it. Maybe it was because I was what we now call a returning student at a time when there were few such students. Being older I was allowed to secure a room in the home of someone rather than live in the residence halls. I also had to work numerous hours each week to pay for my tuition, room and board.

All of these factors contributed to my having few friends among the student body. I found my community among the eight-ten international students on campus, five of whom were Spanish speakers. Thanks to those five students and a young Spanish teacher who was close to my age, I became quite fluent in Spanish.

I taught for two years in southeast Kansas and then applied for and received a Fullbright scholarship to study for a year in Latin America. God works in mysterious ways. My advisor at Emporia State University had suggested that if I applied for countries where few people wanted to go, I would have a better chance of getting a scholarship. So I applied for El Salvador, Bolivia and Paraguay. In March of 1965 I was notified that I had been awarded a grant to study at the Universidad del Valle in Cali, Colombia. It was the only place in Latin America where I knew someone. A girl I had counseled at camp with one summer was married to an Argentine evangelist named Luis Palau and they lived in Cali. I also had history classes at Tabor with a woman who was a missionary in Cali, Built in community!! Not true.

I found my community with the Catholic Colombian family with whom I lived, with classmates at the university and with the young people at the church I attended where Hugo Zorrilla was pastor. Why didn't I find community with the missionaries or the Palaus? I don't know. Maybe it was because I knew I had only a year in which to acquire the language and the culture to the degree possible so I wanted to spend all my time speaking Spanish and avoiding English. Some missionaries accused me of "having gone native" which hurt me deeply and drove me away from encounters with them.

That year changed me profoundly but it would take me another year to discover how much. When my scholarship ended in June of 1967, I returned to the States having signed a contract to teach Spanish in Bethany, Oklahoma, in September. Bethany had an M.B. church and there were people I had known at Tabor. Built in community, right? Yes and no.

For those of you too young to remember, the mid-sixties were the height of the Civil Rights Movement. I had started to pay attention to it during my first two years of teaching, but only intellectually. My experience in Colombia had given me a new worldview; I was better able to see institutionalized racism—the prejudice and discrimination that was built in the fabric of our society, unfortunately even in the church. I grew up with my own set of stereotypes and prejudice but at Tabor I had had to deal with some of them.

Remember I said my community at Tabor was among the international students. One of those international students was a black Colombian; his brother was one of my best friends at the San Fernando Church in Cali. He was the one straight arrow who would always explain cultural mores to me when I broke taboos or when I couldn't understand certain conduct among Colombian friends. I always saw Tono when I saw the beatings of black protesters on TV.

In April Martin Luther King was assassinated and my roommate and I actually feared for our lives. The first encounter was with the principal and fellow teachers who were talking in the teachers' workroom when we came in. "Too bad they didn't get Rap Brown and Stokely Carmichael as well" was the principal's comment. No matter what we said about violence only begetting violence, we were shouted down. Students stopped in our rooms between every class to call us "nigger lovers." The president had ordered the flag be flown at half-mast in honor of Dr. King. Students went out and raised it. The janitor lowered it and the students raised it again. When the janitor started out to lower it again, the principal came on the loudspeaker and announced that at Western Heights the flag would not be flown at half-mast in honor of no N.... By the end of the day, my roommate and I knew we would not be safe at our apartment that weekend. We drove by there, threw a few things in a suitcase and drove to Kansas for the weekend.

About that same time there was talk of building a low-income housing development in Bethany and the church people called a special business meeting to discuss the matter. That meeting was a pivotal point in my life spiritually and professionally. What the church members saw as protecting their property values, I saw as blatant racism. I accused them of being able to send missionaries to Africa but being unable to sit in the same pew with a black American. I was told I wasn't a property owner so I didn't understand. I walked out of the meeting quite disillusioned. I didn't fellowship regularly in a church again for seventeen years.

In May when school let out, I took my roommate to Cali to introduce her to what I had missed all year—my community!! We spent a month and then we returned to Emporia State to finish my Master's degree in Spanish. I had been promised a teaching assistantship for the fall. Instead when I walked onto campus I was offered the position of Foreign Student Advisor. The woman who had held the position for many years and who was also my advisor had had a heart attack in March and had to retire. A classmate of mine had taken over the position at that point but had now been drafted. I agreed to take it as a part time position so that I could finish up my thesis which was all I would have left after the summer coursework. I was to hold the position for the next two years.

I worked closely with students from 17 countries and saw the kind of discrimination they face in finding housing, getting utilities, etc. The worst part of it was that people I knew from different churches were guilty of that discrimination. Or worse yet, they would welcome the African student to their church but didn't walk the Black American student from the college to attend. I became even more disillusioned, but worse yet I became angry. I found community not among those professing Christianity, but rather among the some 100 international students with whom I worked.

In 1970 I was pretty disillusioned. It was a pretty dark period in American history. I had finished my Master's degree in Spanish but there weren't a lot of jobs available in foreign languages. My friend had survived the Vietnam and was returned to Emporia State to reclaim the position. The incidents at Kent State and on other campuses led me to decide to become an expatriate. Emporia State had an exchange program with a University in Colombia and they were looking for someone from the States to head up a new program they were starting—to train secondary teachers in English. I was offered the position and took it. At that point I gave away most of my possessions thinking I would never return to the States and it was too costly to take it along. I arrive in Bucaramanga in August of 1970 and was to spend the next year and a half teaching English at the Universidad Industrial de Santander.

I had taught for four years in the States and I thought I knew how to teach. But in retrospect I have come to the conclusion that I really learned what teaching was all about during that first semester at the UIS. I was to teach three night classes in the teacher training program plus one class of technical English for

Mechanical Engineering students. I was informed that the textbooks had been ordered but they were being held in Customs and no one knew when they would be released. I had one week to figure out what kind of curriculum I could develop and get ready to meet my 30 very eager students. There were few of the technical and visual aids I was used to in the States such as projectors, tape recorders, or even maps and posters. There was an overhead projector but there were no bulbs for it most of the time. There was me, the chalkboard, and the students. We learned to use the newspaper, magazine pictures, and group activities to help these students learn English. Many of the kinds of activities I now use I discovered on my own during the time I was at the UIS and later at the Universidad Nacional in Bogota.

During the second semester the Student Executive became unhappy with government policies and began holding demonstrations. More than once the university was closed for a week or two and then it would be opened again. I was caught on more than one occasion as I would enter the campus at noon for my first class caught between the militant students marching out and the police marching in. It was not much fun being the sandwich meat between those two groups. Finally just after Easter vacation, the national government closed the university and sent the students home for two months.

We hoped to be able to salvage the semester but no one knew whether that would be possible. Interestingly enough in the midst of all this chaos I had formed a close community with three other Americans who were also teaching English and several of the Colombian professors and their families who had spent two years in Emporia getting their Master's degrees. I tried a few of the evangelical churches in the city but opted to attend mass with one of the professor's wives who was a close friend and with whom I lived for several months.

When in July the university still hadn't opened, I accepted a job in Bogota with a textbook company. I would serve as a consultant to their sales personnel and give workshops throughout the country on teaching English as a Foreign Language. When I moved to Bogota, I was again among strangers. Bogota was a much bigger city than Bucaramanga had been. Finding a place to live was not easy. I had four different addresses within eight months. I traveled frequently—three weeks out of every month from September to January and from March to May. So I was not in Bogota enough to really find a community there although some of my friends in Colombia gave me the names of friends they had and I formed a close friendship with one couple. I also got to know a couple of American couples who were there on the Fulbright.

And the Lord worked in my life even though I was not walking in fellowship with him. My roommate moved out on me and I needed to find someone to share a very expensive apartment in which I spent less than half the month. I found an ad in the paper in English "Roommate wanted. Non-smoking female and a phone number." I called the number and ended up with a Mennonite roommate from Ohio. She had studied at Eastern Mennonite and Bluffton, and came to Bogota on a Junior Year Abroad program and stayed. We would be close for the next three years. We would both marry Colombians, our sons would be born a week apart, and we would both end up in Texas within another two years.

I had been there about six months when I met Clinton. I remember how I met him. One of the sales persons came in one afternoon just furious because he couldn't get this one school to adopt our English textbook. The Head English teacher wanted to know the theoretical rationale on which the book was written. So he asked me to go talk to Clinton. For the next year and a half we were professional friends. He would come into the book room, purchase a book and then come back to talk about it. The school he taught at was about six blocks from the apartment where I lived when I was in Bogota. We often would meet on the street and go have a cup of coffee but we had no romantic involvement until the fall of 1972. I had been dating another guy who taught math at the Universidad Nacional but it had been an on again off again relationship for a long time.

Again as I look back I realize how God had his hand in all of this. Though neither of us was walking in fellowship with the Lord; I was not walking in close fellowship with him, but he still guided me in the selection of a mate. In 1972 my boyfriend had stood me up for my birthday and I was pretty blue. Someone at the bookshop asked me to deliver a book to Clinton at the Camilo which I agreed to. When he asked me how I was, I began crying. I ended up telling him the whole story and he invited me out to dinner. He called me frequently over the next three weeks and took me out to dinner two or three times a week.

We were married in May of 1973 which means we will soon have been married for 23 years. A few days after we were married, the company sent me off for three weeks and I came back to turn in my letter of resignation. I took two part-time positions, teaching English. One at the Universidad Nacional and the other at the Pedagogica. Within two months each had evolved into full-time positions. I resigned one of them at Christmas time and would spend the next four years at the Nacional where I had some of my best teaching experiences. Unfortunately, in 1977 the university system in Colombia was convulsed in strikes again and we decided to leave Colombia. By that time we had two lovely children: a son and daughter.

Again God's hand was directing our lives. When we got to my mother's home in Nebraska, there was a contract to teach English in the Rio Grande Valley of Texas. Though I had interviews scheduled for a couple of weeks later in Chicago, we decided a bird in the hand was worth two in the bush and I signed it and we moved to Weslaco, TX. Jeremy was three years old the day we moved into the apartment; our youngest was fifteen months old. There we started attending the Mennonite Brethren Church and the Lord brought my husband and me back into fellowship with Him.

Finding community in South Texas was not easy. Again race

became the issue. My husband, though Colombian, was not considered a Latin by the Mexican American community and he was too black to be accepted by the White community. We stayed there two years. We had friends from our days in Bogota who were now at San Diego State. They encouraged us and so we put our furniture in storage, packed up a few things in the trunk of our 75 Rabbit and came to California.

Part of what made us leave south Texas was Jeremy's asthma which was very severe. We had asked God for direction. If Jeremy's asthma cleared up we would know that California was where we should be. It did so I resigned the position I had in Texas without yet having a position in California. We rented a house in National City and immediately found a church where we felt at home. On Friday before school was to start on Monday, I signed a contract with the Sweetwater Union High School District to teach English and ESL at Sweetwater High.

In 1984 we were making plans to return to Colombia so that our kids could become bilingual and bicultural. I had a contract lined up with a bilingual school in Bucaramanga when I was recruited to the joint doctoral program SDSU had with Claremont Graduate School. Clinton encouraged me to go for it —said I needed to quit collecting Master's degrees.

For the next four years we lived apart. The first year he was in Colombia and the kids and I were in Chula Vista. The next year he had the kids and I was alone at Claremont. The following year we were all together in Santa Marta, Colombia. The next year I was back here to finish up my dissertation and the kids joined me in the spring. It would take another two years to get my husband's green card renewed so that he could join us.

When I received my Ph.D I came to the Valley to teach for two years at Cal State Stanislaus. We chose to live in Merced rather than in Turlock. In August of 1990 I joined the faculty of Fresno Pacific College in education. I commuted from Merced for the first two years and we then moved here in 1993. These six years have been wonderful. I indeed have found community here at

FPC. We are active in Mennonite Community Church. I think I have finally begun to put down some roots. My husband says we are not moving again anytime soon so my 43rd mailing address will have to be during my sabbatical next year. We are hoping to spend the spring of 1997 either in Colombia or in Costa Rica, again finding community among strangers.

ADDITIONAL PHOTOS

A young Mary Ann.

Jeremy and his dad, enjoying life outside institutional walls.

My first visit with Clinton, only a few months after he moved. I was visiting from Germany for a different reason, but was grateful to spend time with him.

Clinton enjoying the Caribbean Sea with his son.

Years later, Jeremy enjoying the same sea with HIS son.

Jeremy, Mary Ann, and Clinton at the sea.

Mary Ann with her lopsided smile, not too long before her death.

Our therapy, Daisy, and Mary Ann's grandson, born with her blue eyes.

Jeremy and I.

Visiting with Daisy in her "new" home 6 years after our move to Germany

Visiting with Daisy in her "new" home 6 years after our move to Germany

Made in the USA
Middletown, DE
26 September 2020